FLEET
THE FLYING YEARS

FLEET
THE FLYING YEARS

Ron Page and William Cumming

THE BOSTON MILLS PRESS

Canadian Cataloguing in Publication Data

Page, R.D. (Ronald David), 1925–
    Fleet: the flying years

Includes bibliographical references.
ISBN 1-55046-019-6

1. Fleet, Reuben Hollis.   2. Sanderson, Jack, 1898–
3. Fleet Aircraft of Canada – History.   4. Aircraft
industry – Canada – History.   I. Cumming, Bill.
II. Title.

HD9711.C2F44 1990   338.7'62913334'0971338   C90-095543-0

Published in Canada by:

THE BOSTON MILLS PRESS
132 Main Street
Erin, Ontario N0B 1T0
(519) 833-2407
Fax: (519) 833-2195

American Association
for State and Local History
Award of Merit

Winners of the
Heritage Canada
Communications Award

Designed by John Denison, Erin
Cover Design by Gill Stead, Guelph
Typography by Lexigraf, Tottenham
Printed by Ampersand, Guelph

Drawings by Bill Bishop and colour profiles by Peter Mossman

The Publisher gratefully acknowledges the assistance of
the Canada Council and the Ontario Arts Council.

TABLE OF CONTENTS

ACKNOWLEDGEMENTS

We would like to acknowledge the following people for their assistance and generous donation of material, photographs and research.

Bruce MacRitchie, the major driving force behind the book who built up the company's records and photo collection from donations made by many retirees and employees.

Terry Judge, who gave so generously of his own research material on Jack Sanderson and the aircraft data of the early thirties, also gave sound editorial advice on details which we would have overlooked.

Fred Shortt of the National Aviation Museum has researched and written many articles on Canadian aircraft in preparation of his own book on the subject, and graciously supplied both material and photographs for this project.

My co-author, Bill Cumming, who helped us over the difficult aircraft sections.

My wife, Bette, patiently encouraged me in the production of the manuscript. Her editorial comments were most helpful.

We also wish to thank the various people who contributed photographs, material and help such as Bill H.Near, Trevor Meldrum, San Diego Aviation Museum, Ross Zimmerman, the late Jack McNulty, Gwyn Morgan, Gord Hill and Fleet Industries. In particular Peter Mossman for the beautiful side-view paintings and Billy Bishop for the three-view drawings.

FOREWORD

"To Bruce from Doug on your 10th birthday 1944" is written on the inside cover of a book entitled *War Planes of the World*. This was my introduction to aviation in the forties, a gift from my brother Doug in the RCAF. My interest in aviation was kept alive and growing with other books, pictures and, during his furlough home, bike rides in the Toronto area to Gillies Field, Barker Field and the Island Airport.

In 1955 I started into aviation with an introductory flight in a Fleet Model 80 Canuck at Central Airways in Toronto. At that time Fleet was just a name, and little did I realize that someday I would have the privilege of working for Fleet in Fort Erie, Ontario. As time progressed I was pleased to purchase CF-DLC Fleet 21 biplane, which I have since donated to the Canadian Warplane Heritage Museum. My family still owns a Fleet Canuck, and that plane is now flown by my children.

During my career at Fleet, I was extremely fortunate to meet with the sons of Reuben Fleet, Sandy and David. For Fleet's 50th anniversary I had the privilege of heading up a small group of volunteers restoring a Fleet-produced PT26A Cornell aircraft, *The Spirit of Fleet II*. I regret that my brother Doug, who worked on the restoration, did not see the "first flight" because of his untimely death in his Stinson aircraft. Since 1982 a volunteer group at Fleet has been restoring a Fleet Fort aircraft, *The Spirit of Fleet III*, owned by the Canadian Warplane Heritage Museum. As part of Fleet's 60th anniversary in 1990, we plan to fly this most interesting and historical aircraft.

It is with much pride and pleasure that I write this foreword for the book *Fleet: The Flying Years* in memory of my brother Doug.

Bruce MacRitchie
November 1989

– Archie Hood Photography Ltd.

PREFACE

The history of Fleet is a long one made up of many stories of the people involved and the products they built. When I started this project, I intended to structure the book in the form of a normal history, but quickly became swamped by the number of aircraft, the stories and the diverse products manufactured by the company over a period of 60 years. The Fleet Aircraft Company alone deserves its own book. I have, therefore, elected to simplify my task by recording the Fleet's history in chronological form, giving a short history on the two major players Major Reuben Hollis Fleet, the founder, and Captain Jack Sanderson, the famous Canadian pilot and first president of Fleet, who was instrumental in laying the foundation of Fleet Aircraft. All the aircraft built by Fleet in Canada are recorded. The majority of the aircraft data was supplied by Fred Shortt of the National Aviation Museum, Ottawa, and I drew heavily from the book written by Ken M. Molson, and H.A. Taylor, *Canadian Aircraft Since 1909*.

I quickly found that the detailed models and variants of the aircraft were not easy to identify and record with accuracy, therefore I co-opted Bill Cumming to become a co-author on the aircraft sections. Terry Judge, of the Canadian Aviation Historical Society (CAHS), was most generous with his knowledge and supplied the majority of the material on Jack Sanderson, as well as other associated Fleet information which he has collected over the years. Terry also edited material on the Sanderson years and the associated aircraft for inaccuracies. The notes made by Jim Carmichael, from his talk to the Ottawa chapter of the CAHS on this subject, were most useful for documenting the turbulent postwar years. Bruce MacRitchie of Fleet Industries, himself a well-known aircraft restorer, historian and pilot, was a major driving force in getting the book written, and a major contributor of material, which he painstakingly collected, after the complete archives of the early Fleet company history were intentionally destroyed in the early 1950s, probably for poor economic reasons to save filing space.

We have purposely limited the book to the Fleet aircraft as they left the factory and have not recorded their individual histories, except in a few cases.

The gestation of this book has been a protracted one, for various personal reasons. Any errors or omissions are ours, but we hope they are not numerous.

It is best to warn the reader now, that anybody who tries to trace the history of Fleet aircraft will quickly find that there is a bewildering array of model numbers and variants due to engine changes and aircraft design modifications. Also, to compound the problem, the original company Consolidated Aircraft, the independent subsidiary Fleet Aircraft Inc., and later Fleet Aircraft of Canada, all used the same assignment of model numbers with different intents and loosely controlled the variant designations. The reader should not be surprised if he or she becomes momentarily confused or finds inconsistencies.

Ron Page
Oakville

Major Fleet beside the Curtiss Jenny in his flying suit with map in May 1918, when he was organizing the first air mail service. – *San Diego Aviation Museum*

I

INTRODUCTION

THE EARLY LIFE OF MAJOR REUBEN HOLLIS FLEET
AND CONSOLIDATED AIRCRAFT COMPANY

It is only appropriate to start the history of the company called Fleet Industries by tracing the early history of the man who formed the company, and whose name the company carries, Reuben Hollis Fleet[1].

Reuben Fleet was born on March 6, 1887, in Montesano, Washington Territory, where he lived with his sister Lillian and their father and mother David and Lillian Fleet. David Fleet was the City Engineer and was heavily involved with real estate. Unfortunately his real estate business collapsed in the Panic of 1893. The Fleet family then returned to their plantation in Virginia, where David Fleet was able to recover the family fortunes and his business. The family moved back to Montesano later, Reuben Fleet's father slowly prospered once more as a real estate agent.

After graduating from the Culver Military Academy at Lake Maxinkuckee in northern Indiana, Reuben Fleet followed in his father's footsteps, rapidly achieving success as a real estate and forestry agent in Washington state. But his early association with the military had made a lasting impression on him and he chose to serve with the National Guard during the formative years of his business career. It was his involvement with the Washington State National Guard that led to his discovery of San Diego as a place he would like to live if he could arrange his business life to achieve it. Unfortunately, this would not happen until 24 years later, in 1935 when he would move his Consolidated Aircraft Company from Buffalo to San Diego.

Reuben's first brush with aviation occurred at age 27, when he obtained a ride with Terah T. Maroney in his flying boat. He immediately became an avid convert to aviation and flew whenever he could.

Through his position as a member of the Washington State Legislature, he was able to influence the federal government to make a significant monetary appropriation for the new U.S. Army Signal Corps Aviation Section. He did this by proposing that the Washington State Legislature appropriate more money for the State National Guard Aviation section. This sum of money was greater than the total approved by Congress for the whole country's Army Signal Corps, Signal Aviation Section. The result was that Congress finally approved $13,281,666 for the new Aviation Section of the U.S. Army Signal Corps. The federal government also offered to train at least one pilot from each State National Guard in 1916.

Reuben Fleet was to benefit from this program when he joined the Army on April 5, 1917, to become a pilot. He started his training at the newly established airfield at North Island near San Diego. He was slightly older than the rest of his class, but graduated with the rank of major, completing his training on Curtiss JN-4D "Jennies" at the age of 30, on August 8, 1917. This title of major would be used by Reuben and his compatriots for the rest of his career.

---

1   Reuben Hollis Fleet's life and his involvement with aircraft is well documented by William Wagner in his book *Reuben Fleet and the Story of Consolidated Aircraft.*

Major Reuben Fleet soon became involved in the pilot training program, the newest American air arm, testing new aircraft and developing test methods and equipment. During this period Fleet accidentally became a fully qualified balloonist when the balloon in which he and two other airmen were receiving instruction was unintentionally released, without the pilot aboard. Reuben took charge of the balloon and they made it back across the Potomac River from Virginia and landed near Washington after a nine hour flight. The qualification to be a pilot in those days was an eight-hour flight without assistance from a balloonist.

One of the flights performed by Reuben as a test pilot was the second test flight of the re-engined, Liberty-powered de Havilland DH-4 at South Field, Dayton, Ohio. The first aircraft had crashed because of a loose spark plug jamming the controls. Both test pilots aboard had been killed. At the end of his test flight, Reuben demonstrated the aircraft with a display of aerobatics, finishing with a spin recovery at 800 feet!

In 1918 he was appointed officer-in-charge of the newly formed Aerial Mail Service on the recommendation of his friend and benefactor Colonel "Hap" Arnold. The War Department had contracted this new service to the Aviation Section of the Army. It had been proposed in a political hurry and was poorly planned and equipped. At that time there were no aircraft suitable for the proposed routes, as none were capable of flying non-stop from Washington to Philadelphia or from Philadelphia to New York. The politicians nonetheless demanded that the service proceed. The first flight took place on May 15, 1918, using Curtiss JN-4H biplanes. The flight almost did not take place as announced, as Major Fleet had to fly the aircraft from Philadelphia that morning, leaving at 08:40 and arriving at the Washington, D.C., Polo Grounds at 10:35. President Woodrow Wilson was there and many other prominent people were in attendance, including 36-year-old Franklin Delano Roosevelt. But Reuben Fleet and his staff could not get the aircraft engine started. It was eventually discovered that someone had forgotten to fill the gas tank after the Major had landed. Once the plane's tanks were refilled, the pilot, Second Lieutenant George L. Boyle was finally able to take off on the first airmail service flight. Unfortunately, he lost his bearings due to the poor visibility and confusion with his compass, and flew south instead of north. He made a forced landing in a ploughed field near Waldorf, Maryland, 25 miles south of the capital, and broke his propeller in the landing. After a second attempt, which also resulted in a forced landing, the mail went by truck and train to Philadelphia. However, Major Fleet and Benjamin Lipsner persevered and were finally successful in getting the service operational. Fleet then turned the Aerial Mail Service over to the Post Office and returned to pilot training duties. Rueben travelled overseas to England with Colonel Hap Arnold. He familiarized himself with the British method of training pilots, which he found superior in every respect to the American method. This new training method was devised by Lieutenant Robert Smith-Barry of the Royal Flying Corps at Gosport. One item of equipment which impressed Fleet was the Gosport tube. This speaking tube allowed the instructor and student to communicate with each other without the aid of electronics[2].

After the Armistice, Major Fleet continued in the Army as a contracting officer and business manager of the Air Service Engineering Division at McCook Field, Dayton, Ohio. He flew whenever he could, but his real objective in staying in the Army was to be able to specify and design a safer and better training plane. Even though he became familiar with the aircraft industry and the service procedures for ordering and specifying aircraft, he was not able to satisfy his personal objective.

---

2   As an embryo pilot I remember using this Gosport tube when learning to fly the de Havilland Tiger Moth at RAF grading school at Marshals Field, near Cambridge, in 1943.

On November 30, 1922, at the age of 35, he left the Air Service Engineering Division of the U.S. Army to start a third career as an aircraft manufacturer. Fleet was offered jobs by both William E. Boeing of Seattle and Clements M. Keys of Curtiss Airplane and Motor Company, but he accepted a third offer, by Edson Fessenden Gallaudet, and became Vice-president and general manager of the Gallaudet Aircraft Corporation. It was not long before he took over the remains of this company and acquired the design rights of trainer planes produced by the Dayton-Wright Company. With only $25,000 in capital, Fleet launched his own company, the Consolidated Aircraft Corporation on May 29, 1923. He used the facilities of the Gallaudet Corporation at Greenwich, Rhode Island, and hired some of its employees. The capital included $10,000 he had borrowed from his sister Lillian.

The first order for this new company, received 11 days after it was formed, was for 20 aircraft of the Model TW-3 side-by-side trainer for the U.S. Army. Although the order was completed, neither Fleet nor the Army was satisfied with this trainer due to the lack of visibility caused by the side-by-side arrangement.

Fleet obtained the service of Colonel Virginius E. Clark when he obtained the Dayton-Wright plane designs. Colonel Clark had been Dayton-Wright's chief designer since 1920. Clark was the designer of the famous Clark Y aerofoil, and he produced an improved trainer for Consolidated which won the new trainer design competition in the summer of 1924. The company received an initial order for 50 of these new aircraft.

This trainer was designated PT-1 and was called the Trusty. It was powered by an uncowled American built Hispano-Suiza 180-horsepower water-cooled V-8 engine. The U.S. Navy initially preferred that the aircraft be powered by a 200-horsepower Wright J-4, and finally with a J-5 nine-cylinder air-cooled radial engine of 220 horsepower. This engine gave the aircraft better lines and became the classical Fleet look. The Navy version of the PT-1 was designated NY-1 (N for Navy and Y for Consolidated, as Curtiss had the C). It was named the Husky.

CONSOLIDATED HUSKY

It is worth recording some of the facts on the Consolidated Husky, from which the Husky Junior was developed. In 1928 Consolidated records showed the following.

"There were more than 700 Consolidated Huskies in service. They had flown over 15 million miles — four times as many as any other type in service in the United States, during the previous ten years. Over 4,000 students had received training on it, more than all the other types combined since World War I. There had never been a fire in a Husky on the ground, or in the air. Many Huskies recorded 1,000 hours — 75,000 miles — without overhaul, better than any automobile.

"The Husky and its derivatives were adopted for standard training by the U.S. Army Air Corps, Naval Air Service, National Guard, Marine Corps, Organized Reserves, Naval Reserves, Cuban Army Air Corps, Brazilian Naval Air Service, Peruvian Army Air Corps and the Siamese Army Air Corps." (The RCAF used Consolidated Couriers.)

To obtain the space and the necessary pool of skilled machinists, Major Reuben Fleet moved his company to Buffalo, New York, on September 22, 1924. He took a ten-year accordion lease on the government-built Curtiss plant. This type of lease allowed him to expand and contract the manufacturing space as the orders for aircraft fluctuated. Both the Army and Navy versions of this trainer, the PT-3 and the NY-2 respectively, were developed from the experimental versions XPT-2 and XPT-3. These later versions used new wing panels incorporating the Clark Y aerofoil. In 1928 Consolidated had delivered 310 of these Husky trainers to the Army and Navy (the Consolidated Model 12 was the commercial derivative of the Husky). The Naval version had a single main float with two wing-tip floats.

Before continuing the story of the evolution of the Fleet trainers, it is interesting to note what Major Fleet and Consolidated were doing in other aircraft fields. (These activities would have an impact on Canada when Canadian Vickers, later Canadair, built the Consolidated Canso or Catalina during WW II.)

When Charles A. Lindbergh flew solo from New York to Paris on May 20-21, 1927, American's interest in flying reached new levels. From 1927 to 1928 the number of passengers carried by the airlines increased from 8,661 to 47,480 people. The number of certified pilots increased from 1,572 to 4,887. This climate was made to order for the prospering young Buffalo company, which wished to expand into the commercial market while also constructing heavier military aircraft.

Fleet's opening move was to employ one of the Air Corp's foremost civilian engineers, I.M. (Mac) Laddon who had designed the GAX attack plane in 1919 and the all-metal CO-1 in 1921. He was also the co-designer of the Bendix-Laddon disc wheel and integral brake.

Mac Laddon joined Consolidated in March 1927. He and his staff were based in downtown Dayton, after being refused permission to set up shop at Wright Field. (One member of his staff was C.B. Carrol, who a quarter century later became the project engineer on the Navy-Convair experiments with the first vertical-takeoff plane, the XFY-1.)

Laddon's initial design involvement was a collaborative effort between Sikorsky and Consolidated. Though the Consolidated Sikorsky Guardian bomber was built, it did not meet specifications and was withdrawn from the Army's heavy bomber competition. It was flown by Leigh Wade of *Around the World* fame of 1924. (Wade served as Vice President of Consolidated from 1928 to 1933.) The team then moved from Dayton to Buffalo to start work on a design for a Navy competition which called for a large flying boat. It was to have a wing span greater than 80 feet and be capable of carrying at least 750 gallons of fuel. This would enable the aircraft to fly non-stop from the west coast to Hawaii.

Laddon also designed a twin-engine monoplane of 100 feet span, having an all-metal hull. This configuration was derived from the Navy's transatlantic NC ("Nancy") boats of 1919. The plane was rushed to completion at Buffalo in December 1928. Since both the Niagara River and Lake Erie were frozen, the plane was crated on flatcars and transported by rail to the Washington Naval Yard for assembly.

The XPY-1 was first test flown on January 10, 1925, with Lieutenant A.W. Gorton at the controls. On January 22, 1929, it was demonstrated to the Assistant Secretary of the Navy for Aeronautics, E.P. Warner, from the Anacostia River, with Lieutenant W.G. Tomlinson at the helm. Though the Admiral (as the XPY-1 was called) won the design competition, Consolidated lost out to Glenn L. Martin Company on the production order, as the Martin Company was the lowest bidder. Fleet was disappointed in losing the production order, but he quickly turned his attention to developing a market for his new flying boat. The outcome was the formation of a partnership to explore the possibilities of developing a New York – South America Airline. The partners consisted of Major Fleet, James H. Rand Jr. (of Remington Rand fame) and Captain Ralph O'Neill. Fleet and Rand put up $15,000 each, and O'Neill contributed his knowledge of aviation and Spanish. By obtaining mail contracts, the NYRBA Line was formed, with the initials standing for *New* York, *Rio* and *Buenos Aires*. NYRBA used 14 of the Commodore Flying Boats, which put Consolidated on the map as makers of big flying boats. The Commodore was an Admiral Model 16 converted to a 22-passenger transport seaplane with two drawing rooms and a crew of three. NYRBA later sold out to Pan American Airlines at a handsome profit. Consolidated continued developing this type of aircraft which became the Ranger series P2Y-1, P2Y-2/3. This last version had the engines mounted on the leading edge of the wings and with streamlined nacelles. This Model P2Y-2/3 was used by the U.S. Navy and led finally to the PBY/Catalina/Canso of WW II.

HUSKY JUNIOR

With the success of his trainers for the U.S. Armed Forces, Fleet looked to the civil market for further expansion. His first try at this market was stillborn because of the poor design of the Consolidated Model 10, a high-wing monoplane with a triangular fuselage, designed by Joe Gwinn. Even though it had several innovative features, the design was not right. Fleet withdrew it before obtaining certification. He decided to turn to his popular military trainers as a model for the design of a smaller, lighter civilian aircraft. Early in 1928 he called four of his key people together and told them to pack for a week's trip. They were George Newman, factory manager; Leigh Wade, test pilot; Joe Gwinn; acting chief engineer and Ralph Oversmith, materials supervisor. They drove to the Buffalo Athletic Club and over the week sketched out the Junior version of the Husky, with a wing span of 28 feet versus the original Husky's 36.5 feet. It was to weigh less than 1,000 pounds and be powered by a Warner Scarab 110-horsepower engine. The first Model 14 Husky Junior was rolled out and test-flown in November 1928. The original prototype had interconnected cockpits like a bathtub (this was later modified into two separate cockpits with a fairing). The design foreshadowed Fleet's future independence from Consolidated. Approximately a dozen Husky Juniors were built. The first aircraft was built in 26 days, and three of them were flown to a Chicago aeronautical fair, where two were sold for $7,500 each.

The following description of the Husky Junior was taken from a Consolidated publication.

CONSOLIDATED HUSKY JUNIOR

General Features of Design and Construction
    The Husky Junior is a two-place, dual control, single-bay biplane with a wing span of 28 feet.

Wing Cellule:
    All metal structure except laminated spruce spars.
    Fabric covered.
    Airfoil – Clark Y – 15%.
    Interplane and centre section streamlined steel tubular "N" struts.
    Two flying wires and one landing wire on each side.

Ailerons:
    On bottom wing only
    Balanced and differential controlled.
    Patented control – no exposed operating parts – eliminates pulleys, bell-cranks and torque tubes.

Fuselage:
    Welded steel tubing – no tie rods.
    Patented 3-point engine mount.
    Cockpit section sturdy alloy steel, fabric covered.

Landing Gear:
    Divided – axle type.
    Heat-treated axles.
    Oleo-spring shock absorbers – 7 in. stroke.

Tail Skid:
    Steel tube – swivel type.
    Oleo-spring shock absorber – 6 in. stroke.
    Patented quick-demountable shoe.
    No openings in rear fuselage fabric, thereby eliminating nuisance of dirt, weeds, etc. collecting in fuselage.

Tail Surfaces:
    Stabilizer adjustable in flight from both cockpits.
    Fin adjustable on ground
    All surfaces – welded steel.
    Fabric covered.

Controls:
    Complete dual.
    Aileron and elevator – stick and push pull tubes (no cables to wear).
    Rudder – pedals and cable.
    Stabilizer – cable and screw.
    Control stick – heat-treated alloy steel tubing.
Power Plant:
    Warner "Scarab," air-cooled 7-cylinder radial engine, 110 hp
    Priming system.
    Heywood starting system (optional).
    Oil System
    One tank – forward of fire wall.
    Normal capacity – 2 gallons.
    Total capacity including expansion space – 3 gallons.
Fuel System:
    One tank – in upper wing.
    Gravity feed.
    Capacity – 24 gallons.
Safety Factors:
    United States Approved Type Certificate Number 84.
Furnishings:
    Dual controls – demountable stick, and rudder pedals infront cockpit.
    Parachute-type seats.
    Leather cushions (life preservers).
Miscellaneous:
    All steel parts protected by 2 coats of aluminum enamel and protected with cadmium plating and all tub-
    ing hermetically sealed.
    All wood parts protected by 3 coats of spar varnish.
    Replaceable bronze bushings and important bearings fitted with high-pressure grease lubricators.
    All bolts in wing spars fitted with bakelite bushings inserted in reamed holes, for extra load bearing
    area.

SPECIFICATIONS

Dimensions:		Data:	
Span	28 ft.	Number of Seats (Dual Control)	2
Length	20 ft. 9 in.	Weight Empty	976 lb.
Height	7 ft. 10 in.	Useful Load	649 lb.
Wing Area-IncludingAilerons	195 sq. ft.	Total Weight	1625 lb.
Wheel Tread.	64 in.	Wing loading (fully loaded) per sq. ft.	– 8.3 lb.
		Power loading(fully loaded) lbs per hp	– 14.75 lb.

General:	
Wing Chord	45 in.
Aspect Ratio	7.5
Angle of Incidence	0°
Dihedral	4°
Wheels	20 x 4 in.

Performance:	
High Speed	110.5 mph at 1940 rpm
Cruising Speed	90 mph
Stalling Speed	35 mph
Radius of Action	360 miles
Fuel Consumption	15 mpg
Ceiling	16,000 ft.
Rate of Climb @ S.L.	930 fpm.

The Consolidated Model 14 Husky Junior c/n 7 with the bath-tub like cockpit, January 1929.
– B. MacRitchie Collection

During this period, Major Fleet's investment bankers were getting ready to go public with Consolidated company shares. The directors and the bankers were nervous about this new, untried product. They were also concerned about the amount of money Fleet was investing in it, and voiced their disapproval. Major Fleet became annoyed at their lack of confidence in his design, and for the sum invested in the Husky Junior, $173,000, he bought the new trainer's rights from the other directors and renamed it the Fleet.

Reuben Fleet formed a new company, Fleet Aircraft Inc., in February 1929 as a sort of personal subsidiary to produce this commercial trainer. He then contracted with Consolidated to manufacture 110 of his planes, so the two companies were still working under the same roof. The Warner-powered Fleet was known as the Fleet Model 1. When W.B. (Bert) Kinner, of Kinner Airplane and Motors Inc., heard about this new aircraft, he went after their engine requirements. Fleet subsequently bought 1,000 engines and purchased 240,000 shares in Kinner's company. With the Kinner engine, the trainer became the Fleet Model 2. The new aircraft sold well, and more than 300 Fleets were delivered in 1929. The Army and Navy rushed to buy it, even though Fleet did not think it was ready for their service. When the other directors of Consolidated saw that the U.S. Armed Forces were going to buy the little trainer in such large numbers, they wanted to buy back in. So after only six months, Major Fleet sold Fleet Aircraft Inc. and 5,000 shares of Kinner Airplane and Motors Inc., plus stock in National Flying Schools and land he had purchased in Canada back to Consolidated Aircraft. This transaction may have taken place in late July or early August 1929. The land that he had bought in Canada in the summer of 1929 was meant to be his solution to the annoying problem of obtaining export permits from the U.S. government. The permits were often delayed and were never issued for sufficient lengths of time. Fleet therefore planned to eventually build a factory in Canada, where he could assemble his aircraft for export.

For now, he was back with Consolidated, a richer man looking across the border to expand his production without the irritating restrictions of the U.S. State Department. All he needed was the right man to run the company in Canada.

The Fleet Model 3 NC443K with
the Wright J-6 five cylinder engine,
August 1929. – *B. MacRitchie Collection*

A close-up of a Fleet 2 with a
long range belly-tank and the
unique undercarriage struts
with an unknown intrepid avia-
tor, either Wade or Wheatley,
August 1929.

– *B. MacRitchie Collection*

Fleet aircraft on display at Cleveland Air Show, September 1929. – *B. MacRitchie Collection*

II

FIRST DECADE 1930-1939

MAJOR FLEET AND THE SANDERSON YEARS

The stage was set for the birth of Fleet Aircraft of Canada Ltd. Fleet and Consolidated had an aircraft, the Husky Jr., now named the Fleet Model 1 & 2, or simply Fleet 1 & 2, and it was selling well in the civil market. However, the company was frustrated by U.S. export permits, which the State Department would issue for periods of no longer than three months. This caused considerable difficulty, as the materials for any one order had to be procured 18 months ahead of delivery of the aircraft. This was evidently not a new problem for Reuben Fleet, as he had already been looking across the border for a solution. He had bought some property near Fort Erie, Ontario in the Township of Bertie, near Amergari, on July 8, 1929, with the idea of starting a Canadian plant. The property was the northern half of Lot 4 Concession No. 4, consisting of 50 acres, and the northern half of Lot 4 Concession No.3, consisting of 49 acres at the corner of Gilmore Road and Pettit Boulevard and west of the Erie Downs Golf and Country Club.

Though land clearing, tree removal and grading took place in July and August 1929, as did the removal of a house on the property, no formal work on the construction of the plant occurred until the spring of 1930.

The pieces all came together at the end of a 15,000-mile, month-long sales trip, when Fleet and his secretary had a forced landing and crashed in Ontario during the last leg of the trip. The day was Friday the 13th, September 1929.

Fleet always flew his own Fleet aircraft, and on this long sales trip he had decided to take his secretary, Mrs. Lauretta Lederer Golem, along as co-pilot. In fact she had started to take flying lessons in preparation for the exciting trip. The trip went well and the new Fleet 3 (Wright J-6 engine) trainer was well received. It was not until the final leg of the return journey, from Detroit to Buffalo, that trouble occurred. Reuben had decided to take the land route over Ontario rather than the more hazardous over-water route across Lake Erie.

Mrs. Golem was at the controls in the back seat as they flew over West Lorne, when the trusty Whirlwind lost power due to a valve rocker arm failure, and Fleet took over the controls. He tried to make a forced landing, but unfortunately he stalled and crashed into the field of farmer Russell Reid. Both pilot and co-pilot were seriously hurt, Mrs. Golem with a broken neck and Reuben with multiple injuries. Mrs. Golem died the next day. Reuben was very distraught when told of her death.

It was while Reuben Fleet was hospitalized at the Victoria Hospital in London, Ontario, for seven weeks that he met Captain W.J. (Jack) Sanderson.[1] Jack Sanderson was a former pilot with the Royal Air Force and was well known as a pilot across Canada. Sanderson visited Reuben out of kindness to a fellow pilot, not knowing it was to change the course of his life. Sanderson was to play a significant part in the formation of Fleet Aircraft of Canada Ltd.

William John (Jack) Sanderson, born on November 24, 1898, was the youngest of four boys in a family of six children. He was raised on a farm outside London, Ontario, and was a bit of a daredevil as a lad. During long winter evenings he would ride bareback hell-for-

---

1   Material originally researched and written by Terry Judge.

leather through the deep snow, knowing that they would probably hit a high unseen drift, whereupon both horse and rider would somersault into the snow. The game was that if the horse got out first, it would race home, leaving the rider to struggle home as best he could.

When the Great War came he followed his three brothers into the Canadian Army. In 1916 he was with the 9th Battalion Canadian Railway Troops (CRT), whose task was to build light-gauge railway lines from a base behind the lines right up to the trenches where the fighting was most active. Sanderson was assigned to drive a Ford truck. He spent his time ferrying officers, survey parties and wounded soldiers, back and forth to the front. He was constantly under artillery fire and threat of gas attack. Unfortunately, he was caught in the tailend of one which, although not severe, was enough to hospitalize him for a few weeks. When he returned to his unit, Sanderson became more and more intrigued with the aircraft that patrolled and fought over the lines. In mid-1917 he requested a transfer from the horror and filth of the ground war to the more glamorous Royal Flying Corps (RFC). This was granted and he was transferred to England for training. During Jack's first familiarization flight, his instructor tried to impress him, but instead hit a tree and badly damaged the aircraft. Fortunately, neither pupil nor instructor was seriously hurt. Jack progressed successively from the DH-6 to BE-2e, BE-2d, RE-8 and DH-4 aircraft. Shortly after the RFC became the Royal Air Force (RAF) he graduated with the grand total of 35 flying hours to his credit and was posted to No. 110 Squadron based at Bettoncourt, where he flew the DH-9A and participated in several bombing raids. The interesting feature of these raids was the high altitude at which they were flown, some 20,000 feet. Following the Armistice, the squadron moved to Maisoncelle and participated in the pioneering airmail service for the British Forces. The mail was brought across the Channel, sorted, and then delivered by No. 110 Squadron to the units garrisoned along the Rhine.

When the squadron disbanded in August 1919, Sanderson returned to Canada and his father's farm at London, Ontario. Later he found employment as a mechanic and an automobile test-driver with the London Motors Ltd., which manufactured the London Six, a high-quality limousine. Unfortunately, the company went bankrupt in 1924, the same year that Jack and Gladys were married. Jack then took over his father's farm on the 4th Concession near London. There, the couple eked out an existence as market gardeners, growing strawberries, asparagus and other vegetables, with a few greenhouses.

In mid-1927 the government announced that it was preparing to encourage the creation of civilian flying clubs. From one end of the country to the other, like-minded individuals gathered to organize themselves in preparation for whatever the government had in mind. London was no exception, and Captain Jack Sanderson was soon involved in the organization of a flying club.

With the publication of the *Standard Conditions for Light Aeroplane Clubs* by the government in September 1927, the embryo organizations moved into high gear to finalize all details. The London Flying Club was incorporated in April 1928 and Sanderson was chosen as the club flying instructor. That same month he reported to Camp Borden for the instructors' course, but because so many other potential instructors from around the country had already reported, the commanding officer regretfully had to turn him away. However, in May, he was asked to report to the de Havilland aerodrome at Weston, outside Toronto, for his course. There he received his Commercial Air Pilot's certificate on July 13, 1928. By the end of July 1928 the London Flying Club was in business with two DH-60 Moths.

The London Flying Club was not the busiest in Canada. During the week, flying was mainly confined to the early mornings and evenings, thus allowing Sanderson to work the farm during the rest of the day. He used the aircraft whenever he could on business and pleasure. During April 1929 he tendered his resignation to enter a business privately teaching flying at London Airport. This project did not materialize, as he was still with the flying club in September. The story continues in Captain W.J. Sanderson's own words:

"During the period when I was the manager and chief flying instructor at the London Flying Club, a Fleet Model 3 biplane crashed just south of the airport. The plane was badly wrecked and one of the occupants was the pilot, Major Reuben H. Fleet, owner of the company which manufactured the plane. He was badly shaken up, and his secretary, who had been riding in the back seat, died of her injuries. As one pilot to another, I went to the hospital to visit with Major Fleet. After I told him who I was, he started to tell me who he was. This was quite a long oration, which ended by him looking straight at me and saying with great pride, 'I guess you have heard of my name?' Not being a bit impressed, I said the wrong thing at the wrong time: 'I never heard of you.'

"It seemed that the shock of the remark was almost as bad as that of the crash itself. He left me thinking that he must be some sort of a nut. Three days elapsed before I went in to visit the Major again. To my surprise he seemed most pleased to see me. Right away he started to talk. 'Jack, I have decided to sell the Canadian Air Force my Fleet trainer. I would like you to tell me what is the right way to go about it.' I replied, 'Well, Major, first, you would have to hire a Canadian pilot to be your Canadian representative. Second, import one of your planes into Canada, paying all duty and taxes, so it could be registered with Canadian markings as a demonstrator. The pilot would then fly it around the country, visiting the flying personnel at the RCAF stations and the civilian flying clubs. The reception of the Fleet trainer, favourable or otherwise, would be reported to you. At that time you would have to decide whether you want to go ahead with entering the Canadian market. If you do, then to sell to the RCAF and the government-sponsored flying clubs, you would have to provide the facilities in Canada to manufacture the plane.'

"The next day when I visited him, he told me that the plan I had outlined was a good one and that he had decided to go ahead with it. At this point he offered me the position as his Canadian representative — which I did not accept! He was very annoyed with me for not jumping at the chance of accepting the opportunity of working for the great Major Reuben H. Fleet. He then asked me why. I replied, 'Major Fleet, if I accepted your offer it would change my whole life. I have not seen your factory nor the plane, and we Canadians do not jump overboard without knowing the details. Therefore, before I could give you my decision I would want to visit your factory and fly the plane.' He was annoyed and grabbed his phone at his bedside and called his office in Buffalo. He instructed someone to come to London, pick me up, show me the factory, let me fly the plane, and then bring me back to London. When I returned to London, I was thrilled but tried to act as nonchalant as possible. I informed the Major that I would take the job."

Thus began what would turn out to be a frequently tempestuous relationship!

FLEET AIRCRAFT OF CANADA LIMITED

Once this agreement to work together was finalized, progress started to happen fast in the birth of Fleet Aircraft of Canada Ltd. Sanderson handed in his resignation at the London Flying Club, then the first demonstrator was imported at the end of October 1929. It was a Fleet Model 2, registered as CF-AKC. Sanderson flew it around Ontario, where it was well received, even though the effects of the recent stock market crash were evident everywhere. Later he contracted Jim Holley of Winnipeg to demonstrate the trainer in various parts of western Canada. This allowed Sanderson to concentrate on organizing the new company and getting the factory built.

Letters patent were granted for the new company, Fleet Aircraft of Canada Limited, on March 25, 1930. On April 10 Austin Company began erection of the steelwork for the 7,200-square-foot plant at Fort Erie. It was just three miles across the river from the parent

The front of the original Fleet plant 1930, Fort Erie, Ontario.

Rear of the original Fleet factory, early 1930s. The St. Catharines Flying Club's DH60 Moth CF-CAW was flown by Mrs. M.E. Camm, wife of well-known Fort Erie druggist. – *Ross Zimmerman Collection*

The Fleet plant in 1982, the original Fleet building is just across from the water tower.
– *B. MacRitchie Collection*

company. The building was 60 by 120 feet., consisting of machine shop, offices, assembly area and a storage shed to house four to five planes. It had a brick front with corrugated steel walls and cost about $25,000. Fleet Aircraft of Canada Ltd. was a wholly owned subsidiary of Consolidated Aircraft. Captain Jack Sanderson was its president and general manager. It was a very beneficial arrangement for some of the 400 Canadian Consolidated workers who had previously crossed the Peace Bridge to work in the U.S.A. every day. Also the two companies arranged with the Canadian and American governments to accept the validity of their invoices as they moved materials and equipment back and forth across the border by land and air. This trust was never broken and Reuben Fleet said he would not have broken it for a $100,000.

As the plant's completion was delayed by a month due to bad weather and the poor road conditions to the site, it was not ready until June 1930. The one order that Jim Holley had obtained in Vancouver had to be filled from the American parent company's production line. To accelerate the plant start-up, several pre-assembled fuselage frames were shipped across from the Buffalo plant, and the aircraft were assembled in Canada.[2]

FLEET MODEL 2

Most of the aircraft produced during Fleet Aircraft of Canada's first years of operation were Model 2 trainers. The Canadian prototype was CF-ANL, first flown at Fort Erie on June 27, 1930, by Jack Sanderson. The first Consolidated Model 2 was imported in October 1929 as a demonstrator and registered as CF-AKC. (It was later replaced by CF-AOC as Jack's favourite demonstrator aircraft.)

The construction of the Model 2 was conventional and came out of the same stable as the Husky Junior (Consolidated Model 14 or Fleet Model 1). It consisted of a fabric-covered welded-steel fuselage and metal panels forward of the cockpits. It had steel-tube fairing formers and wooden stringers. No wheel brakes were fitted and, like the early de Havilland Tiger Moths only a tailskid was provided for dragging the aircraft to a halt.

The wings were of equal spans, single bay and wire braced. The upper wing was made in one piece and was constructed with two solid spruce spars. Ailerons were found only on the bottom wings. They were operated by a mechanism of tubes and levers enclosed in the wings and ailerons. Stamped aluminum-alloy ribs were used to construct the wings, and steel-tube compression struts were at the interplane and centre section of the wings. Interlaced between the wings were streamlined landing and flying wires.

The Fleet Model 2 was a very good trainer and had excellent flying characteristics. Its rugged strength inspired confidence in the *ab initio* pilots.

A total of seven Fleet Model 2 aircraft were built in Canada for civilian operators. After that, production switched to the Model 7. Two of the Model 2s were sold in British Columbia (CF-ANL/ANN). The other aircraft were registered as CF-ANM, ANO, AOE, AOF and ATO.

---

2   The U.S. Fleet production list has a gap of only 7 construction numbers at this point of time. Three of these have been identified as having been used at Fort Erie. It is assumed that the other 4 were also used.

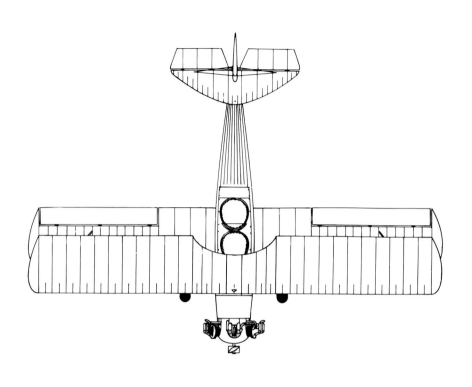

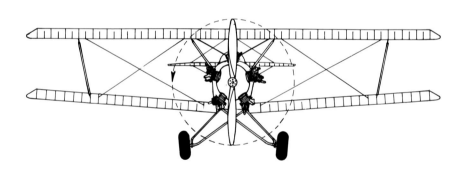

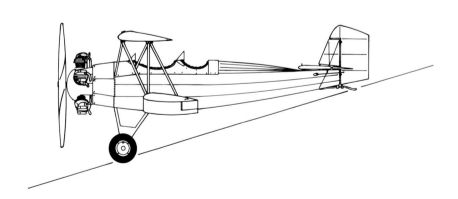

FLEET 2

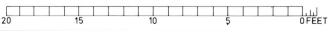

20   15   10   5   0 FEET

FLEET MODEL 2 DATA

Engine:
    100 hp Kinner K-5, five cylinder radial
Dimensions:
    Wing Span – 28 ft.
    Length – 21 ft. 8 in.
    Wing Area – 194.4 sq. ft.
Performance:

Wheels		Floats
Max. Speed @ sea level – 110 mph		– 101 mph
Cruise Speed @ sea level – 95 mph		– 85 mph
Rate of climb – 730 ft/min.		– 584 ft/min.
Service ceiling – 14,700 ft.		– 12,500 ft.

Weights:

Wheels		Floats
Gross Weight – 1575 lb.		– 1761 lb.
Empty Weight – 1023 lb.		– 1252 lb.

The year 1930 was a special one for Jack Sanderson and Fleet Canada. Not only did Sanderson try out the Consolidated Fleetster Model 20 for Major Fleet, but he also was testing new aircraft and flying his new demonstrator CF-AOC. The CF-AOC was then sent to Ottawa for extensive testing and evaluation, by the RCAF, and this evaluation resulted in the RCAF placing an order for 20 Fleet trainers, the largest single order for Canadian-built aircraft placed by the RCAF to that time. It was also the year of the first Fleet float-plane test, on September 2.

FLEET MODEL 7 FAWN I & II

The Fleet Model 7 trainer became the standard production model. It was essentially a Model 2 with a more powerful Kinner 125-horsepower B-5 engine. In all other respects, initially, it was identical to the Model 2. Almost immediately, however, the small fin of the Model 2 was replaced with a larger fin. The larger fin became standard on all Canadian Model 7s, and the few aircraft which were manufactured with the small fin were retrofitted with the larger version. Wheelbrakes were optional on the Fleet 7 and a tail-skid or steerable tail-wheel was offered.

The Model 7 was the first Fleet trainer to enter service with the Royal Canadian Air Force. The initial order was for 20 aircraft and all were delivered during 1931. They were known as Fawn Is by the military, carrying RCAF serial numbers 190-209. (To be technically correct, the name Fawn only came into being during WWII.) Later in the 1930s, as the international situation deteriorated, four additional batches of Fawns were ordered, totalling 51 aircraft for the RCAF . The final 31 aircraft were delivered as Fawn IIs (Model 7C), from 1936 to 1938. In addition, 12 civil-registered Kinner-powered Fleet 7Bs were delivered to the Department of National Defence in 1936 for issue to various flying clubs.

During August 1931 one of the Fawn Is delivered to the RCAF was returned to the Fleet factory to be fitted with a de Havilland Gipsy III in-line engine. This new version of the Fleet 7 was assigned the Model 7G (for Gipsy) and was tested by the RCAF during November and December 1931, and by Consolidated Aircraft in the United States in January 1932. It received favourable reports on its performance, but was never put into production in Canada; Consolidated built a large number for export. The airframe was eventually refitted with the Kinner B-5 engine and returned to its 7B designation.

The RCAF requested that Fleet Aircraft investigate and fit an Armstrong Siddeley Civet engine to a Model 7. The Civet was the name given to the seven-cylinder Armstrong Siddeley Genet Major engine by the Royal Canadian Air Force. As the Civet rotated in the opposite direction to the Kinner engines, a rudder fin cambered to the starboard was required. This was necessary to compensate for the reverse direction of the torque.

A trial installation was made with the Civet engine, using RCAF Fawn 193. The aircraft was first test-flown in April 1935 and found to be the best of the Model 7s. The Civet was smoother and quieter in operation than the Kinner, and the added power (10 hp) improved the performance of the Fawn. With the Civet engine installed, the basic model designation was the Fleet Model 7C, and with the RCAF it was known as the Fawn II.

Other engine options were offered by Fleet for the series of trainer aircraft — the Kinner K-5, the 125-horsepower Warner Scarab, the 145-horsepower Warner Super Scarab and the Kinner R-5 — but none were built. Optional equipment which could be supplied with the Model 7s included a fuselage belly tank and fixed cockpit enclosure with a hinged side. This was termed a coupé top. The belly tank fitted externally between the undercarriage legs and had a 20-Imperial-gallon capacity. This gave the Model 7 a total capacity of 40 Imperial gallons and an endurance of 7 hours. Only four or five installations of the external belly tank were completed.

The coupé top did not prove to be quite as popular, and only one RCAF and three civil installations were ever completed. The RCAF Fawn aircraft were fitted with sliding cockpit enclosures during the late 1930s This became standard equipment on all RCAF Fawns.

The Model 7s were delivered to civilian flying clubs across Canada and to various RCAF stations. Two were exported, one to Great Britain and another to New Zealand. As spare engine parts for the English Civet engine became increasingly difficult for Britain to deliver during the early stages of the war, it was necessary that all RCAF 7Cs be converted to 7Bs, with the Kinner B-5. This was done by 1940.

Most of the original 20 Fawn Is were on strength with the RCAF at Camp Borden, which was the home of the RCAF main training establishment. From 1937 onwards, most of the Fleets were stationed at Trenton, and some Kinner-powered aircraft were passed on to the Auxiliary squadrons. The Fawns continued to serve in a training role until April 1944.

As with the Model 2, the Model 7 was an excellent trainer and had rugged strength. The RCAF was very impressed with the Fleet Model 7 and claimed that the aircraft was one of the factors which most improved the flying standards of the RCAF .

A total of 71 Fleet Model 2s & 7s have been identified.

FLEET MODEL 7 DATA

Engine:
    Model 7 – 130 hp Kinner B-5R
    Model 7A – 100 hp Kinner K-5
    Model 7B – 130 hp Kinner B-5, five-cylinder radial
    Model 7C – 140 hp Armstrong Siddeley Civet IA, seven-cylinder radia
    Model 7G – 120 hp dH Gipsy III, four-cylinder in-line

Dimensions:
    Wing Span   – 28 ft.
    Length   – Model 7B – 21 ft. 8 in.
                       – Model 7C – 21 ft. 8 in.
                       – Model 7G – 22 ft. 5 in.
    Wing Area   – 194.4 sq.ft.

Performance:
    Max. Speed @ sea level   – Model 7B – 115 mph
                             – Model 7C – 120 mph
                             – Model 7G – 107 mph

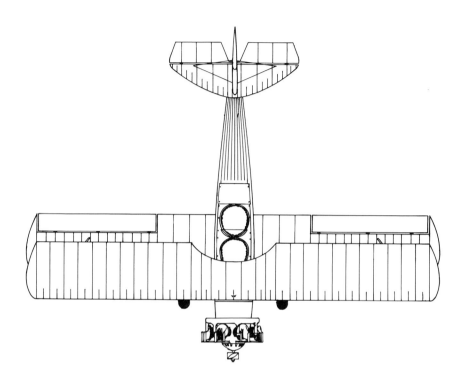

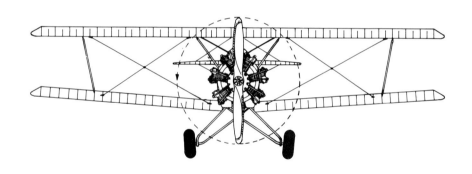

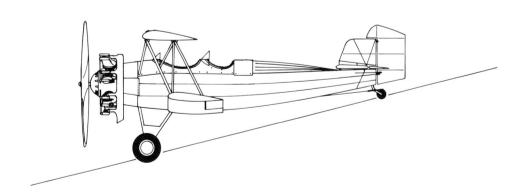

FLEET 7B FAWN

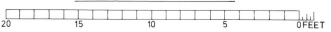

20　　　15　　　10　　　5　　　0 FEET

Cruise Speed @ sea level	– Model 7B – 95 mph
	– Model 7C – 100 mph
Service Ceiling	– Model 7B – 15,500 feet
	– Model 7C – 14,300 feet
Rate of Climb	– Model 7B – 760 feet/min.
	– Model 7C – 765 feet/min.
Weights:	
Gross Weight	– Model 7B – 1,740 lb.
	– Model 7C – 1,860 lb.
	– Model 7G – 1,635 lb.
Empty Weight	– Model 7B – 1,146 lb.
	– Model 7C – 1,220 lb.
	– Model 7G – 1,087 lb.

It would be 1935 before Fleet Aircraft of Canada could make all the components for the trainers in Canada. This was achieved by Sanderson moving all the jigs and equipment left behind by Consolidated when the parent company moved to San Diego. Major Fleet did not find out about this until it was accomplished. It was to stand him in good stead, however, when he sold the company to a Canadian business group in 1936.

In 1931 there were only 11 employees at Fleet Canada. Sanderson had four former members of the London Flying Club working for him; they had all been taught to fly by Jack. Fred Sims was an expert mechanic, Russell Busch was in charge of the radio bonding, Jack McGinnis was in charge of the cover department, and Ab Silcox was factory superintendent.

The Trans Canada Flying Pageant took place in 1931, travelling across Canada and back. Starting at Hamilton, it flew out across the prairies to British Columbia, and then all the way east to the Maritimes before finishing back at London, Ontario. Jack Sanderson with his Fleet demonstrator CF-AOC logged over 375 hours flying on this trip. He was able to boast that it cost less than $10 for repairs. He had fitted the aircraft for limited inverted flying, for which he became well known.

On returning from the tour Jack Sanderson found that the outlook for the company had worsened with the deepening recession. There were no new orders for aircraft, only the overhaul of several Fleets for both the RCAF and civilian customers. There was some excitement when the Western Canada Airways Consolidated Fleetster CF-AIP was trucked in from the West for repairs. This was a similar model to the one which Sanderson had flown in the States at Major Fleet's request. The Fleetster was a high-wing monoplane, with the then new stressed-skin monocoque fuselage construction. It was an advanced design for its time and was called the Model 20 by Consolidated.

By 1932 there were only eight full-time plus two part-time workers at Fleet, and the outlook was pretty bleak. The Major finally phoned to tell Sanderson to close the place down. He carried out Major Fleet's instruction by paying his employees what they were owed and giving them each a week's vacation pay. What he did not tell the Major was that he had hired them all back on to finish the various jobs that were going through the factory. Nevertheless he had to lay them off permanently a short time later.

It was during this period that Sanderson and Major Fleet arrived at a revised method of operation. First, Jack would stop living on the premises and thus save the company on insurance premiums. Secondly, Major Fleet would pay him the princely sum of $75 per month. Jack was still in the aircraft business but unfortunately there was no business. Though, to judge by his appearances at the various airshows on the summer circuit, you would have assumed everything was going well. His Fleet demonstrator CF-AOC was always prominent, particularly in his distinctive style of aerobatics both right-side up and up-side down. On March 8, 1933 Jack Sanderson was recommended for the Trans-Canada or McKee Trophy for 1932.

First Fleet – manufactured Fleet 7 with standard coupé enclosure with Sanderson in front cockpit, who was also the firms test pilot. He used CF-AOC extensively for flight demonstrations. – *Terry Judge Collection*

Fleet 2 on floats November 31, 1929, the first Canadian demonstrator. Note the unusual spacing of the registration. – *NAM 10641*

Fleet Fawns for the Royal Canadian Air Force and Model 2 outside the back of the Fleet plant, 1930. – *B. MacRitchie Collection*

A group photo of early Fleet employees standing in front of Fleet 7B CF-CER. It was purchased by DND for the Montreal Light Aeroplane Club in 1936. – *B. MacRitchie Collection*

Fleet 2 CF-ANF on floats doing an engine run-up, Vancouver, 1938. – *Jack McNulty Collection*

Fleet 2 CF-AOF Hamilton Airport, November 7, 1944. Note the unusual exhaust pipes.
– *Jack McNulty Collection*

Col. W.A. (Billy) Bishop V.C. in front of a Fleet 2 CF-ANG at Montreal Light Aeroplane Club, Cartierville, Quebec. – *NAM 3572*

Fleet 2 CF-ANO on floats with coupé top, Arrow Airways, Flin Flon, Manitoba.
– *National Aviation Museum (NAM) 14805*

Fleet Fawn with 155 hp Kinner engine restored and operated by Canadian Warplane Heritage Museum, Mount Hope, Hamilton, Ontario. – *Bill Cumming Collection*

The Fleet Model 2/7 as obtained by Canadian Warplane Heritage from Scott Smith, Orlando, Florida in its red and white paint scheme. It was built in 1929 by Consolidated and later modified to a Model 7. – *R.D. Page*

Fleet Fawn I RCAF 198 Model 7B with blind flying hood installed on the rear cockpit.
– Jack McNulty Collection

RCAF 208 Fawn I Model 7B modified with the sliding canopy at Camp Borden June 4, 1938.
– Jack McNulty Collection

Fleet Fawn 7C RCAF 280 Fawn II on skis at Camp Borden October 10, 1940.

– Jack McNulty Collection

The only Fleet Model 7G converted by the RCAF, serial No. 193, with a de Havilland Gipsy Major III engine. *– NAM 13404*

WACO ZQC-6 Fleet demonstrator CF-BDW *Miss Sweet Caporal*, MacDonald Tobacco Sales Company of Canada Ltd, June 1937. – *B. MacRitchie Collection*

WACO ZQC-6 CF-BDP, Aylmer 1942. – *M.L. McIntyre Collection*

WACO

During 1933 Sanderson started to collect ideas for an ideal bush plane. He sent out a questionnaire to all companies associated with northern bush flying. From the answers to this survey he was able to get a good idea of what the market wanted. (Fleet had already done overhaul jobs on aircraft like the Fairchild FC-2W2 (CF-AOU), Curtiss-Reid Rambler (ex CF-CCB), Fleet CF-ANG, and DH60X Moth G-CAUB, which were used for bush flying.) He first considered the Fokker Universal, as well as the Stinson, but finally selected the Waco four-placed cabin biplane. Sanderson obtained the Canadian rights to this aircraft in early 1934. He cooperated with Arcier, the designer, to adapt the Waco to northern Canadian conditions and to make it into a bush-plane taxi-cab.

Initially the aircraft was fitted with the Continental engine for which Sanderson was the Canadian distributor. In late 1934 it was mated with the Jacobs engine, which started a long and profitable relationship between Sanderson and Al Jacobs. The first Waco arrived at Fleet on March 29, 1934, for final fitting. Fleet completed 14 Waco conversions during 1935 and also became the Canadian agency for both Jacobs and Kinner engines during this period. The Waco registered as CF-BDW was used by Fleet and Sanderson as a demonstrator. It was put up for sale in January 1938, but was not sold until 1946. The remains of this aircraft were stored at the Canadian Warplane Heritage Museum, Mount Hope Airport, and were donated to the museum by Bruce MacRitchie. The remains were sold in 1989 to the Reynolds Aviation Museum, Wetaskiwin, Saskatchewan for restoration.

WACO DATA

ENGINE:
    Continental and Jacobs L-6

DIMENSIONS:
    Wing Span – 35.0 ft.
    Length – 25.7 ft.Wing Area – 244 sq.ft.
    Wing Area – 244 sq. ft.

The economy started to pick up in 1934, but it was still hard going to obtain any sizable orders. Sanderson was able to coerce Consolidated into sharing a production order with Fleet Aircraft of Canada for trainers for China. This order consisted of 30 Model 10 aircraft for Colonel Jouett's mission and 6 for the Cantonese Air Force.

FLEET MODEL 10

The Model 10 was developed after some spinning problems in the United States. It was this problem that led to the development of the Consolidated Model 5 and 10 (the latter was also the Canadian Fleet Model 10). The aircraft had a deepened rear fuselage, which was built up by fairings over the standard structure. This necessitated a two-piece tail-plane which was divided by the fuselage, and a new fin and rudder were fitted. The undercarriage was redesigned completely, with the wheels being moved forward by 6.5 inches, to allow for wheel brakes. A steerable tail-wheel was also fitted.

The Chinese order was completed about May 1935, and was comprised of 30 Model 10Bs (Consolidated Model 10), along with parts and materials for 20 more, and 6 Model 10As (Consolidated Model 5) for the Cantonese Air Force. It is assumed that the aircraft production was shared 50/50, so 15 Model 10Bs and 3 Model 10As were built in Canada, plus at least 10 others that were supplied as parts and materials.

Meanwhile, Fleet had improved the Model 7 by installing the undercarriage from the Model 10 on the Model 7s. They continued to market the Model 7 in this form and adopted the new-design Model 10 as their export model, but made no attempt to sell it in Canada until 1938. The Model 10 with various engines, was sold to Argentina (20), China (18+50), the Dominican Republic (2), Iraq (1), Mexico (5), Nicaragua (1), Portugal (16), Venezuela (6)

Fleet Model 10B with Chinese markings. – *B. MacRitchie Collection*

A Venezuela export aircraft Model 10D. – *NAM 5326*

Fleet Aircraft of Canada Ltd. production line, while they were producing the Chinese aircraft.
– *B. MacRitchie Collection*

Model 10-32Ds E-2, 3, 4, 5 ready for Mexico at Fort Erie, Ontario, 1936. The one in the foreground serial E-1 was built in the States. – *NAM 14681*

Production line at Consolidated Aircraft, Buffalo, of the Model 10G, September 9, 1934.
– *B. MacRitchie Collection*

and Yugoslavia (2), for a total of 121 rather than 160 aircraft, as it is believed that c/ns 212 to 240 were not built.

The most interesting variant of this aircraft type was the Model 10-32D, the long wing-Fleet. This variant was produced for Mexico with a 32 foot wing-span, which was four feet longer than the standard Model 10 wing. The bigger wing span was necessary to permit normal operations from the higher altitudes of the Mexican airfields. The Mexican order consisted of a U.S.-built prototype and five Canadian-built examples. Two other Model 10-32Ds were built in the U.S.A.

Three Model 10Bs and three Model 10Gs were supplied as seaplanes on Edo 1835 floats for the Portuguese Navy. An enlarged rudder with an aerodynamic balance area below the fuselage was fitted to these Fleet trainers.

A single Model 10D was built in May 1938 as a Canadian demonstrator and was the only Canadian-registered Model 10. This aircraft was extensively evaluated by the RCAF at Trenton. As a result of this testing, RCAF requested that several modifications be made to the aircraft to make it suitable for aerobatics with full military equipment. The changes included making the wing spars from Douglas fir instead of spruce, heavier gauge tubing for the interplane struts and fuselage members, double landing wires, and double wires on the underside of the tail-plane. With these changes incorporated, Fleet designated this design the Model 16.

Including the single Model 10 built for use in Canada, the total number of Model 10s built in Canada has been identified as 122.

MODEL 10 DATA

Engine:
    Model 10A – 100 hp Kinner K-5 five-cylinder radial
    Model 10B – 130 hp Kinner B-5 five-cylinder radial
    Model 10D & 10-32D – 175 hp Kinner R-5 five-cylinder radial
    Model 10E – 125 hp Warner Scarab seven-cylinder radial
    Model 10F – 175 hp Warner Super Scarab seven-cylinder radial
    Model 10G – 130 hp de Havilland Gipsy Major four-cylinder in-line inverted

Dimensions:

Wing Span	– 28 ft. (all Models except Model 10-32)
	– 32 ft. (Model 10-32)
Length	– 21 ft. 8 in.
Wing Area	– 194.4 sq.ft. (all models except Model 10-32)
	– 254.4 sq.ft. (Model 10-32)

Performance:

Max. Speed @ sea level	– Model 10A – 106 mph
	– Model 10B – 113 mph
	– Model 10D – 124 mph
	– Model 10-32D – 122 mph
	– Model 10E – 118 mph
	– Model 10G – 113 mph
Cruise Speed @ sea level	– Model 10A – 91 mph
	– Model 10B – 98 mph
	– Model 10D – 104 mph
	– Model 10-32D – 102 mph
	– Model 10E – 98 mph
	– Model 10F – 103 mph
	– Model 10G – 98 mph

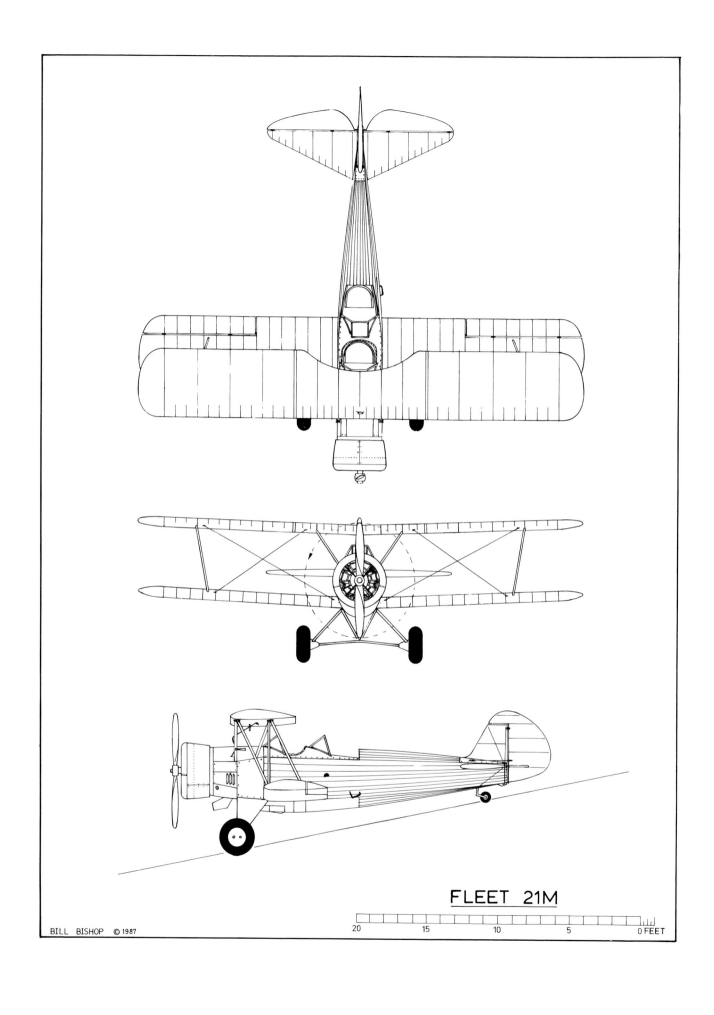

FLEET 21M

20   15   10   5   0 FEET

Model 10G Serial No.79 with the Gipsy Major in-line engine for Portuguese Naval Air Service. – *NAM 14685*

A Model 10B on Edo 1835 floats for the Portuguese Naval Air Service. – *NAM 14683*

Service Ceiling	– Model 10A – 11,600 ft.
	– Model 10B – 15,900 ft.
	– Model 10D – 17,800 ft.
	– Model 10-32D – n/a
	– Model 10E – n/a
	– Model 10F – n/a
	– Model 10G – 14,000 ft.
Rate of Climb	– Model 10A – 640 ft/min.
	– Model 10B – 990 ft/min.
	– Model 10D – 1,100 ft/min.
	– Model 10-32D – n/a
	– Model 10E – 990 ft/min.
	– Model 10G – 800 ft/min.
Weights:	
Gross Weight	– Model 10A – 1,860 lb.
	– Model 10B – 1,860 lb
	– Model 10D – 1,860 lb.
	– Model 10-32D – 1,860 lb.
	– Model 10E – 1,860 lb.
	– Model 10F – 1,860 lb.
	– Model 10G – 1,860 lb.
Empty Weight	– Model 10A – 1,102 lb.
	– Model 10B – 1,122 lb.
	– Model 10D – 1,148 lb.
	– Model 10-32D – 1,200 lb.
	– Model 10E – n/a

One of the highlights of production orders in this period was the placing of an order by the RCAF for ten Fawns in May 1935. But even though the first plane flew in late 1935, it was not until early 1936 that the RCAF would accept them. By July the staff at Fleet had risen to 20, and by the end of the year the employee roster had reached 48.

Consolidated made their long-awaited transcontinental move to San Diego in October 1935. This provided Sanderson with an opportunity to corner the Fleet trainer production market for Canada, as Major Fleet had left behind in storage all the Fleet jigs, tools and special equipment that the Canadian company did not have. As Sanderson had the key to the warehouse, he approached the Canadian Customs to allow him to import this pile of scrap iron in bond so that he could keep his people employed making spare parts. Evidently the Canadian officials were impressed with the idea, particularly with the prospect of increased work and employment. A number of days later a five-ton truck arrived, loaded with the scrap iron, on which Sanderson was only too happy to pay the import duty. It was not until several weeks later that Major Fleet found out that his equipment had been moved from the Buffalo warehouse to the Fort Erie site. Fleet's yell really did not need a telephone to carry it to Canada. The Major demanded the return of the jigs, but when Jack pointed out that the Major would have to pay a very high rate of import duty, he quietened down. Fleet later terminated the previous arrangement and placed all employees back on the payroll. Sanderson went back to being general manager. As the activity at the plant started to pick up, plans were made to expand the Fort Erie plant, even though Fleet Aircraft of Canada had only the Canadian market (worldwide sales were still controlled by Consolidated in San Diego).

FLEET MODEL 21

In December 1935 Consolidated landed an order for ten Model 21s bombing and reconnaissance trainer aircraft for the Mexican Air Force; these were to be built at Fort Erie. This was a major step up from a relatively unsophisticated trainer like the Fawn, and production required the staff to be increased to 47. George J. Newman was sent to Fleet from Consolidated to supervise the building of the Model 21M Wasp-engine trainers for Mexico.

The Consolidated Model 21 was a two-seater trainer, a more powerful version of the PT-11 and PT-12 primary trainers that were in service with the U.S. Army Air Corps. Fleet was promoting the aircraft in Canada as an advanced trainer and designated it the Fleet 21. This aircraft was substantially larger than the Fleet trainers then in production at Fort Erie. The fuselage was made of welded steel tubing and was fabric covered. The wings had wooden spars and Duralumin ribs with fabric covering. The crew consisted of a pilot in the front cockpit and an observer in the rear one.

The Mexican order for the Model 21s was completed in the summer of 1937. The aircraft was powered by the Pratt & Whitney Wasp Jr. engine and was designated the Model 21M. These particular aircraft were also equipped with a forward-firing fixed machine gun, which fired under the front cowling, and the observer's station was equipped with a movable machine gun. Very little is known of the Fleet 21's service in the Mexican Air Force, although photographs of the aircraft show them operating with the front cowling removed.

An additional Model 21M was built by Fleet Aircraft as a demonstrator. During September 1937 this aircraft was flown by a number of RCAF pilots at Rockcliffe, Ontario. At this time the aircraft did not carry a registration of any type. Although the test pilots liked the aircraft and praised its flying characteristics, the Air Force felt the Model 21 was obsolete and unsuitable for the advanced trainer role. This was far-sighted for the Canadian Air Force, considering that two biplanes, the Gloster Gladiator fighter and the Fairey Swordfish torpedo-bomber, were front-line equipment in the RAF and FAA at that time.

Fort Erie was also the location of an Irvin Air Chute factory, which held contracts to produce parachutes for the British Commonwealth Air Training Plan. The contract stipulated that each chute had to be drop-tested from an aircraft prior to delivery. The Fleet 21 demonstrator was converted to a single-seat machine to be used for drop-testing the parachutes. It was flown by Fleet's chief test pilot, Tommy Williams. The rear cockpit was modified by replacing the seat with a cell capable of accommodating two life-size rubber dummies, each weighing approximately 200 pounds. In the first year of operation, the Fleet 21M dropped 3,511 chutes. It did an additional 39 hours in which no record was kept as to the number of chutes tested. Failure of chutes was extremely rare, but occasionally a dummy would slip out of its harness and fall to the ground. To alleviate the boredom of chute-dropping, Williams would side slip the aircraft down and try to land before the chutes reached the ground. During this time, as best as can be determined, the Fleet 21M did not wear RCAF roundels and military serial numbers, nor was any civilian registration assigned to it.

In October 1946 civilian registration CF-DLC was assigned to the aircraft. About a year later the Fleet 21M became expendable hardware to Fleet. It was sold to Tommy Williams, who installed a Jacobs 330-horsepower engine in it. He kept the aircraft on his farm near Woodstock, Ontario, with the intention of converting it to a duster aircraft for his apple orchard, but in the end he used it to perform aerobatic displays at air shows and flew the aircraft just for pleasure. Tommy Williams flew his last aerobatic display at St. Catharines, Ontario on October 1, 1971, at the age of 86, as Canada's oldest licensed pilot. He is reported to have said, "If I hadn't bought the plane [the Fleet 21], it would have been tall grass for me long ago." Bruce MacRitchie bought the aircraft in 1972 and restored it to its original two-seater configuration. It is now part of Canadian Warplane Heritage Museum collection.

FLEET MODEL 21 DATA

Engine:
    Model 21K – 350 hp Jacobs L-6MB, 7 cylinder radial
    Model 21M – 450 hp Pratt & Whitney R-985 Wasp Jr., 9 cylinder radial

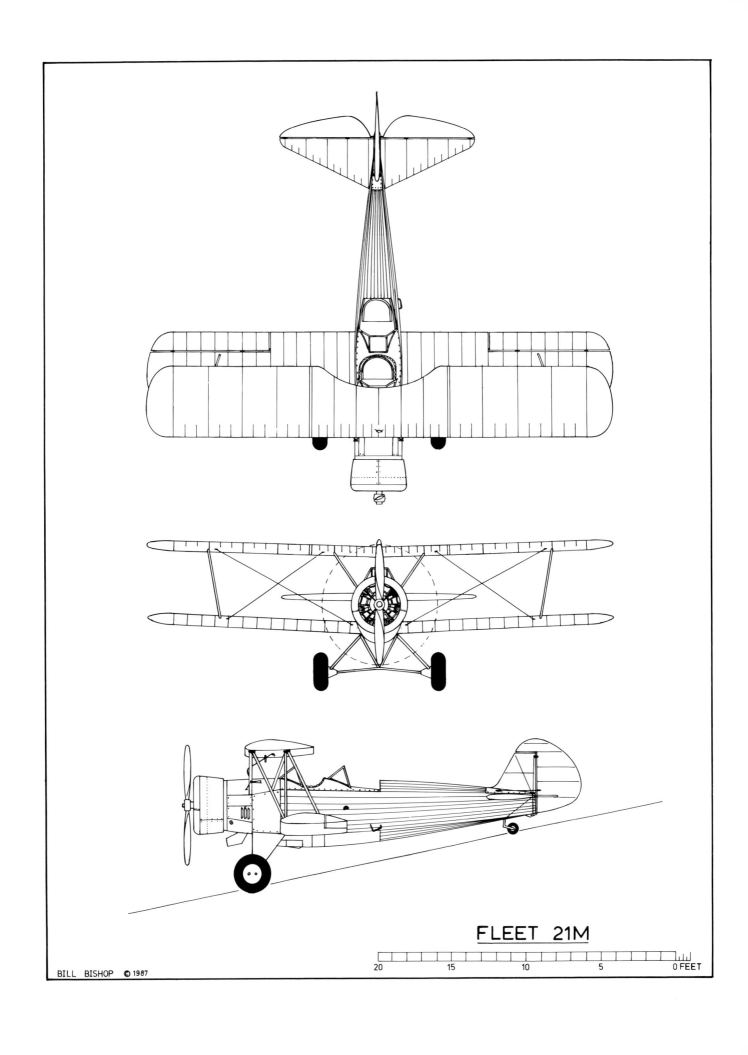

FLEET 21M

20   15   10   5   0 FEET

BILL BISHOP © 1987

This Model 21M was owned by Fleet and used by the chief test pilot Tommy Williams to test drop parachutes with dummies attached for the Irvin Parachute Co. The rear cockpit was faired over with hatch underneath to release the dummies and chutes. The registration CF-DLC-X is used to denote test aircraft. – *Jack McNulty Collection*

Mexican Air Force Fleet 21M No. 27 showing the machine gun mounted in the rear cockpit, with unknown pilot all bundled up. – *Ross Zimmerman Collection*

Tommy Williams in front of his favourite aircraft the Fleet 21K, October 1962.
– *Ross Zimmerman Collection*

A good side view of the Fleet 21, as restored by Bruce MacRitchie to its original two-seater configuration at Fort Erie, 1974. – *Jack McNulty Collection*

50

Dimensions: (both Models)
    Wing Span   – 31 ft. 6 in.
    Length   – 27 ft.
    Wing Area   – 286 sq.ft.

Performance:
    Max. Speed @ sea level   – 139 mph
    Service Ceiling   – Model 21K – 16,500 ft.
                             – Model 21M – 19,000 ft.
    Rate of Climb   – 1,150 feet/min. (both Models)

Weights:
    Gross Weight   – Model 21K – 3,300 lb.
                             – Model 21M – 3,957 lb.
    Empty Weight   – Model 21K – 2,281 lb.
                             – Model 21M – 2,211 lb.

By early 1936 additional orders had started to come in, including more trainers for the RCAF (10 Fawn IIs) and the flying clubs (12), Mexico (5), Yugoslavia (2) and England (1). There was a running battle between the government and the flying clubs, because the clubs were requesting safety harness rather than the simple lap belts. The government's reply was that the clubs did not need the harness, as Sanderson did all his aerobatics and inverted flying with a lap belt. By the time the government finally offered to provide the harness in 1940, the clubs and Sanderson had all bought their own harness.

It is interesting to note that one of the two Fleets that were exported to Yugoslavia became the only Fleet aircraft to see combat duty, as it was pressed into service by the Yugoslavian Partisans during WWII. It was eventually destroyed by the Germans.

Since Consolidated's move to San Diego, the lines of communication had been strained by the distance between the companies. In the summer of 1936 Major Fleet requested a meeting with Sanderson in New York. The Major had decided to sell Fleet Aircraft of Canada to a Montreal stockbrokerage called Nesbitt, Thompson and Co. Ltd. Captain Jack was still to run the company, but he would now have to report to a board of directors. The whole factory, land and equipment were to be sold first for $500,000 but the Major later changed his mind and raised it to $1,000,000. The five tons of scrap iron which represented the jigs and fixtures for the Fleet trainers that Sanderson — had semi-legally brought over the border — had now become a major asset to the company.

FLEET AIRCRAFT LTD.

The deal went through and the company's name was changed to Fleet Aircraft Ltd., effective November 17, 1936. The directors were W.J. Sanderson (president), E.G. McMillan (lawyer, vice-president), A.J. Nesbitt, M.A. Thompson, Major R.H. Fleet, J.M. Gwinn, Air Vice-Marshal W.A. Bishop, H.H. Horsfall (president and general manager of Canada Wire and Cable), and John Irwin (president of McColl-Frontenac Oil Company). Consolidated received cash and shares for the land, and for the manufacturing and marketing rights to the Fleet trainer and the Model 21 (except for America, China and Romania). Sanderson received cash for the rights to the Waco line of aircraft. Fleet Aircraft Ltd. became a wholly owned Canadian company when Nesbitt, Thompson offered 50,000 of the 100,000 authorized shares to the public on January 4, 1937. During this period the plant was expanded to five times the size of the original 1930 plant at a cost of $50,000.

In his new role as president reporting to a board of directors, Sanderson found the working arrangements quite different and sometimes difficult. He was now dealing with hard-nosed businessmen who had very little experience with the aircraft business and whose top priority was the balance sheet.

The prototype Freighter on floats on the Niagara river, 1938. Note the unusual window opening of the cockpit. – *B. MacRitchie Collection*

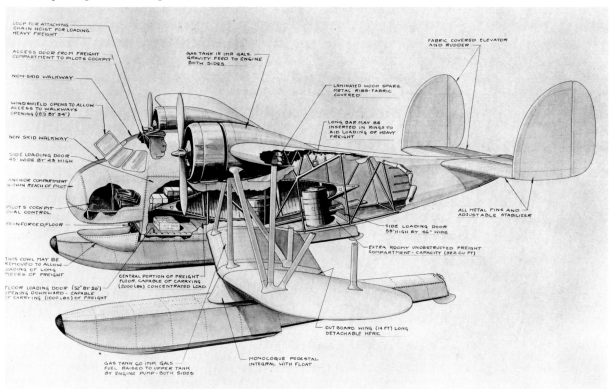

A cutaway drawing describing the Freighters features. – *B. MacRitchie Collection*

In 1937 the company saw an improving market for the Fleet product and orders started to roll in from overseas. These sales were handled through agencies, principally Aviation Equipment and Export Inc. (Aviquipo). The majority of the aircraft produced by Fleet Aircraft Ltd. from 1937 to the beginning of the war were for export to countries such as China (50), Argentina (20), Portugal (6), Venezuela (6), the Dominican Republic (2), New Zealand (1), Iraq (1), America (1), plus another order of 50 for China an order which was cancelled in favour of the Ryan STC-4.

FLEET MODEL 50 FREIGHTER

It was toward the end of 1936 that Fleet President W.J. Sanderson again considered the potential bush-plane market. He was awake many a long night thinking of building a twin-engine aircraft. He felt there was a need to complement the Waco, and other aircraft of this type, with a twin-engine freighter. To see if his ideas were on target, he sent another questionnaire asking the bush pilots about their requirements of a bush-plane. The answers he received were varied, but they helped to confirm some of his ideas and allowed him to lay down the general specifications for Fleet's new bush aircraft. It should have an easy freight-loading access, a short takeoff, and be capable of being dismantled into relatively small components, except the fuselage and floats, in order to facilitate repairs and component replacement in the remote wilderness.

The Fleet Freighter design team, led by Project Engineer R. E. (Dick) Young, consisted of Joe Gwinn Jr. of Consolidated Aircraft and Tom McCracken, Fleet's plant manager. Young, along with Sanderson, completed the layout for the new Freighter aircraft. Gwinn, who had designed the Fleet trainer, completed the stress analysis on the aircraft. In general the design followed Sanderson's concept, with simple rugged construction and a low wing loading for short takeoff.

The Fleet 50 was a strut-braced biplane with engines mounted on the leading edge of the upper wing. The lower wing was an inverted-gull with the undercarriage mounted at its lowest point. The fuselage was of welded steel tubing faired with aluminum hat-section stringers. The fabric was fastened with Parker-Kalon (PK) screws and washers similar to those used on the original Fleet trainers. The cabin floor was heavy aluminum alloy sheet. The cockpit was semi-monocoque construction with a steel tube airframe structure that carried past the cockpit to the nose section to serve as a nose-over structure. The fixed tail surfaces were aluminum-alloy semi-monocoque construction, with the fins mounted at the outer ends of the tail-plane. Twin endplate fins and rudders were chosen so the Freighter could get close inshore on a lake for loading without touching trees. The rear spar of the tail-plane was hinged to the fuselage and braced with streamlined steel struts. The leading edge was adjustable, for trimming the aircraft, by means of a vertical jackscrew operated from the cockpit by an endless cable and wheel, similar to that used on the Westland Lysander.

The landing gear was a fixed tail-wheel type and was interchangeable between wheels, skis and floats. Jacking points on the lower stub front spars permitted change-over from floats, wheels or skis without hoisting the aircraft. The inverted-gull lower wing enabled a special version of the Edo-type floats to be mounted directly to the wing to enable the aircraft to straddle low docks and load through a floor hatch.

Careful attention was paid to the design of the Freighter, to ensure the ease of loading cargo. There was a 46-by-56-inch door at the rear of the cabin on each side, and a 46-by-45 inch door at the front on the port side. There was also, a 52-by-56 inch hatch in the front cabin floor to allow bulky items to be hoisted directly on board the aircraft. This made it possible to load a crated engine up through the cabin floor. The lower portion of the aircraft's nose was removable to permit long items such as pipe and lumber to be easily loaded.

The clean design of the float installation on the Freighter. – *B. MacRitchie Collection*

The nearly complete Freighter CF-BJU under construction on floats.

– *B. MacRitchie Collection*

A close-up of the ski installation on the Fleet Freighter. – *B. MacRitchie Collection*

A view of the instrument panel and control column of the Fleet Freighter. The control column could be swung over to allow the aircraft to be flown from both sides of the cockpit.

– *B. MacRitchie Collection*

The Freighter was intended to use the Jacobs L-6MB engines of 330 horsepower, but until an Approved Type Certificate was issued the prototype was fitted with Jacobs L-5MB engines of 285-horsepower engines. The L-5 engines underpowered the aircraft, but the more powerful L-6 engine proved heavier, less reliable and did not substantially improve the aircraft's performance. Low engine power was to be the Freighter's biggest drawback, as it could not maintain height on one engine with an appreciable load. Fleet Model 50J designation was assigned to Freighters equipped with the L-5 engines, and Model 50K designation was assigned to L-6 engine Freighters.

The Freighter was also offered as a passenger aircraft, with arrangements of six to eight seats of the airline type or up to ten of the bench-seat type. Passenger Freighters were built with different window and door arrangements. The second and third aircraft were built as passenger models, with the elimination of the front freight door, and an extra window was added to each side. A proposed military version, which was never produced, would have had a fixed forward machine gun and two flexible mounted guns at the rear, one on top and the other at the bottom of the fuselage, with internal and external bomb storage. Also offered was a photo-survey model with camera hatch and provision for a Fairchild Photogrammetry 9 x 9 camera, and an air ambulance version with four seats and space for four stretchers or eight seats and room for two stretchers.

The Fleet Freighter was announced to the industry in the spring of 1937. Fleet production found this to be a rather large aircraft, quite a step up in construction from building relatively small, simple trainers. The rest of 1937 and early 1938 was spent on construction of the prototype Model 50J (CF-BDX). At the end of February 1938 the Fleet Freighter was ready to be flown, and it provided a test of Sanderson's ability as a pilot. In his words, "The day came when the prototype was ready to be flown [February 22, 1938]. It was a big day at the factory, as it was not only the first flight, but I was going to — or try to — fly a twin-engine aircraft for the first time. The flight went off in quite an orderly fashion and I could not see why everybody was so excited." In those days there was only a handful of pilots who were qualified to test-fly all types of land-planes, seaplanes and flyingboats. Sanderson was joined in this group by Leigh Capreol, George Spradbrow and Red Lymburner. The notable difference was that Sanderson was also the head of an aircraft manufacturing firm.

The initial flight testing was conducted at the Fort Erie airfield. In April the Freighter was flown to St. Hubert Airport for still further tests at the larger and better-equipped airport. The Freighter was returned to Fort Erie and was immediately put on floats for water-borne trials on the nearby Niagara River.

A temporary Certificate of Airworthiness was recommended on May 11, 1938, after Department of Transport flight tests at Ottawa, Ontario. On September 6, 1939, the Model 50K received a full C.of A. approval for cargo and passenger operation.

Only five Freighters were built and they were not well received by the operators, due to the poor engine performance. The first four were built for civilian operators. The fifth Freighter was completed specifically for the RCAF. All five aircraft had relatively short careers due to crashes or engine fires. The RCAF Serial No. 800 Freighter had the longest life of the five. After little use, it was sold by the RCAF in 1944, and it spent the rest of its life in Mexico as XA-DOE, until it was written off in 1946. The Freighter was doomed from its beginning, mainly due to its unpopular engines and their lack of power. Canada declared war on Germany four days after the Model 50K received certification, ending all hope of ironing out its problems and commencing production. Given more time, Fleet may well have developed the Freighter into a successful aircraft. It was a good design and handled well, but the lack of power gave it a poor acceptance by the bush community, as it could not maintain

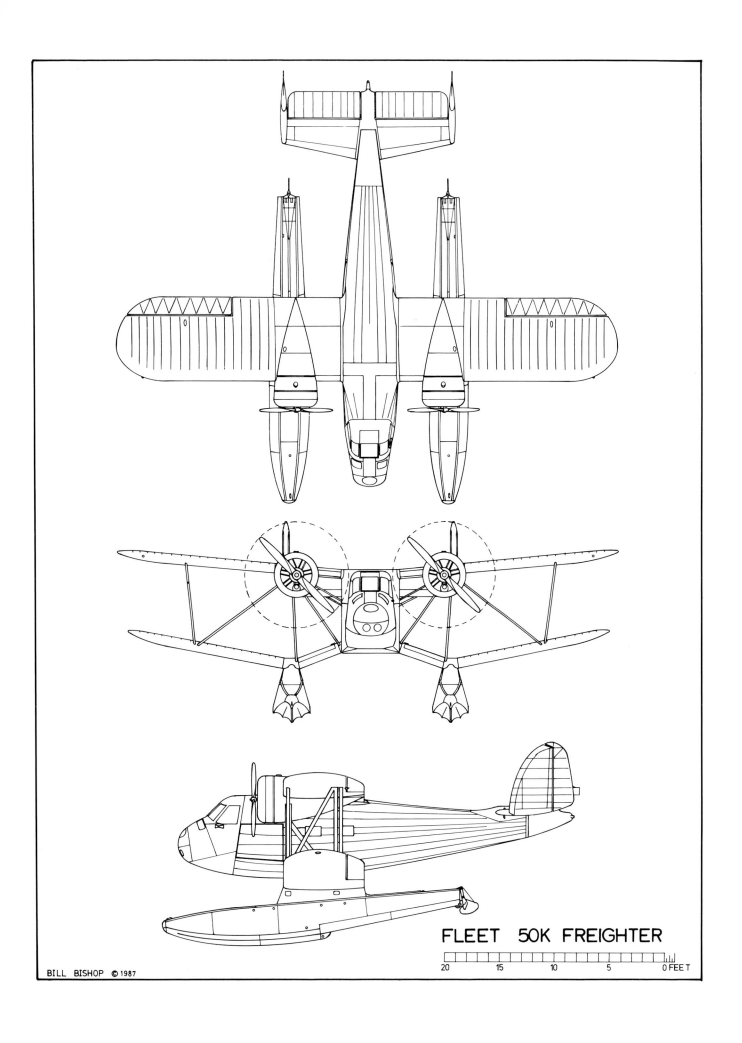

FLEET 50K FREIGHTER

20   15   10   5   0 FEET

height on a single engine. The remains of two Freighter aircraft reside at the National Aeronautical Collection in Ottawa, awaiting future restoration.

FLEET FREIGHTER MODEL 50 DATA

Engine:
    Model 50J – two 285 hp Jacobs L-5MB 7-cylinder radial
    Model 50K – two 330 hp Jacobs L-6MB 7-cylinder radial

Dimensions: (both models)

Wing Span	– 45 ft. (upper)
	– 43 ft. 4 in. (lower)
Length	– 35 ft. 10 in.
Wing Area	– 528 sq. ft. (combined)
	– 268 sq. ft. (upper)
	– 257 sq. ft. (lower)

Performance:

Max. Speed @ sea level	– Model J – 137.6 mph
	– Model K – 150 mph
	– Model K – 132 mph
Service Ceiling	– Model J – 11,500 ft.
	– Model K – 15,000 ft.
Rate of Climb	– Model J – 800 ft/min.
	– Model K – 1,000 ft/min.

Weights:

Gross Weight	– Model J – 8,000 lbs.
	– Model K – 8,326 lbs.
Empty Weight	– Model J – 4,665 lbs. (wheels)
	– Model K – 4,889 lbs. (wheels)
	– Model J – 5,040 lbs. (floats)
	– Model K – 5,121 lbs. (floats)

Note: all five aircraft built had varying weights due to the different equipment installed.

Through the 1930s Sanderson was involved with the Canadian Flying Clubs Association. His duties included awarding of the Webster Trophy to Canada's most outstanding amateur pilot. This award was based on tests in general flying and air navigation. During the 1937 competition Sanderson announced that in future the runner-up in the competition would be the recipient of the Sanderson Shield. The winner of the shield in 1937 was Gordon R. McGregor, later the president of Trans-Canada Airlines. This was a bit of a letdown for McGregor who had won the Webster Trophy outright in 1935 and 1936 and who won it again in 1938.

Fleet Aircraft Ltd. was now producing more aircraft than any other aircraft company in Canada. With the company's increased prominence, Sanderson was appointed to the Board of Directors of the Commercial Air Transport and Manufacturers Association of Canada (CATMAC) in November 1937, in recognition of his abilities as head of a growing aircraft manufacturing company.

A classical view of CF-BDX at its mooring on the Niagara river. Note the large freight door opening. – *B. MacRitchie Collection*

A rare view of the passenger version of the Fleet Model 50K CF-BJT airborne. Note the tailskid instead of a tail-wheel. – *B. MacRitchie Collection*

The Fleet Fort Model 60K prototype, with the semi-retractable spats over the wheels, 1940. These spats were not put into production. – *B. MacRitchie Collection*

Close-up of cockpit area of Fleet Fort I. Student pilot in front and the instructor in the raised cockpit behind. The roll-bar behind the front cockpit has not been fitted yet.

– *B. MacRitchie Collection*

III

THE GATHERING STORM – 1938 – 1939

The years 1938 and 1939 saw an accelerating tempo at Fleet, particularly in Jack Sanderson's daily schedule. He describes these days as the most exciting, hectic and sometimes most frustrating of his life. Exciting because he found himself in the centre of events and privy to the drama that was unfolding in Europe. Hectic because of his many transAtlantic and transcontinental trips. Frustrating, because as a man of action he was intolerant of people who played politics, instead of placing their country's requirements first.

By April 1938 the number of employees at Fleet had reached 165. In mid-April a British trade mission left for America and almost as an afterthought, its members stopped in Canada to investigate the country's aircraft production facilities. At the same time, the Commercial Air Transport and Manufacturers Association of Canada, with Sanderson in attendance, was meeting with the Deputy Minister of National Defence, Major General L.R. LaFléche. In this meeting the association offered its entire facilities to Canada and the U.K. The British trade mission, led by J.G. Weir, a British industrialist, took part in a conference with CATMAC in Montreal on May 18, at which the aims of the mission were presented and discussed. One of the proposals was the formation of a consortium of companies from eastern Canada to manufacture a British-designed aircraft. There was a tentative agreement on this objective. Also, during meetings in Ottawa, discussion took place regarding a possible air training program of pilots for the RAF.

When Sanderson presented the conclusions of the aircraft meeting to his board of directors, they were sceptical, preferring not to make a move until the British came forward with a bonafide contract. Though Sanderson was also concerned with the lack of a firm contract, he was more concerned with the relationship between the British and Canadian governments, as they were not good. In his words, "When I added up all the meagre information I had at that time, it seemed to me there was something in the wind that would probably catch us awfully short in the near future. With this in mind, I put out an order to my staff to start ordering material to make at least 20 trainers. Also, to get started on welding up the fuselages, because this would be the bottleneck when the rush to fulfil orders started."

During this period he had the Model 10 fitted with a more powerful Kinner engine and built as a demonstrator, to be loaned to the RCAF for evaluation. On top of all this the Fleet Freighter needed to be flight-tested and demonstrated to prospective customers. During May a version of the Freighter on floats was launched and test-flown. Then there was the Waco to be delivered to the west coast, with the new Jacobs L-6 engine.

Because of the RCAF's lack of interest in the Model 21, Sanderson felt that Fleet should produce a replacement trainer.: "What I was after was to build an aeroplane that would do as good a job as the Harvard."

FLEET FORT MODEL 60

To meet the new generation of military aircraft which were to appear in the 1940s, Fleet set out to design and produce an all-metal advanced monoplane trainer. The new Model 60 was developed to compete with the North American Harvard, offering significantly lower costs in both production and operation.

Once again Sanderson laid out the aircraft with R.E. (Dick) Young, the aeronautical engineer and test pilot at Fleet, with Joe Gwinn as a consulting engineer. This was an even bigger step than the Fleet Freighter, as this was the first Canadian-designed, all-metal monoplane trainer. It was in fact the only Canadian aircraft designed and built during the war years, as all the other aircraft were built under licence from either the U.K. or the U.S.A. The Fleet Fort was to be an intermediate trainer, but it ultimately served during its service career as a wireless-operator trainer. This was an unglamorous but essential task. It made an important contribution to the war effort as a large percentage of the radio operators trained in Canada flew in the Fort aircraft. The Fleet Fort would fade into oblivion before the end of WWII.

As a private venture Fleet Aircraft Company produced the prototype Model 60. It was powered with the 330-horsepower Jacobs radial engine and fitted with a non-retractable undercarriage, which featured semi-retractable streamline fairings or spats around the wheels. The object of this was to give experience with retractable undercarriage to pilot trainees, without the weight, hydraulic complexity and inherent danger of a conventional retractable landing gear. The instructor's cockpit was placed above and behind the student's cockpit, giving the instructor a good forward view. The monoplane wing design was unusual in two respects: first, the wing was strutted to the fuselage to carry the heavy loads expected from student pilots, as there was no specific centre section, other than a reinforced bulkhead; the second unusual design feature of the wing was the semi-elliptical shape of the trailing edge, with the ailerons extending out to the wing tip. The D-shaped nose spar was an English design, as was the method for attaching the wing fabric to the spar. The design chosen was adaptable to both metal and wooden construction.

Despite the extensive use the RCAF made of the Fleet Model 7 Fawn trainers and subsequent orders the company received for the Fleet Model 16 Finch trainers, the government took no official interest in the development of the Fleet Model 60 Fort. One of the reasons for the lack interest was that the RCAF considered the Fort was unsuitable for advanced training due to its lack of retractable landing gear. Even with the steady issuance of progress reports and sales pitches by the company, the RCAF made it obvious that they had no intention of committing themselves until there was an actual aircraft to test and examine.

On March 22, 1940, Tommy Williams and Dick Young made the first flight test in the prototype. During May 1940, three RCAF pilots performed evaluation tests on the prototype Model 60, now assigned a civil registration CF-BQP, at the Central Flying School in Trenton, Ontario. These pilots were enthusiastic about the aircraft, praising its ground and flying characteristics. They compared the Model 60 directly with the Harvard, noting that its performance was in many ways equal to that of the Harvard. The test officers considered the aircraft to be a suitable intermediate stable trainer with the addition of guns and bombracks.

By this time the war in Europe was deteriorating. It was clear the U.K. might well fall short in its promise to supply aircraft for the Air Training Plan. On the strength of the test report, the RCAF, through the Department of Munitions and Supply placed an order with Fleet Aircraft for 200 Model 60K aircraft, to be used as intermediate trainers. They also agreed to pay for the development and purchase of the prototype trainer aircraft. The name Fort I was selected.

Production was slow to begin at Fleet. The first production aircraft, RCAF No. 3651, flew on May 1941. Once the RCAF got their hands on the Fort I, numerous problems became apparent. The brakes were a continuing source of difficulty, as the Fort became noted for turning over on its back or ground looping due to grabbing or locking by the brakes. In fact, the first time it was taken to Ottawa to be shown off to the senior officials, it ended up on its back when the brakes locked on its landing at Ottawa. There was a hurried repair the night before the demonstration, including the installation of a new canopy which had to be flown up from Fort Erie.

During the initial stages of the war, the RCAF introduced a three-level training program for pilots. Initial flying training was on light aircraft, like the British Tiger Moth or Fleet

Fleet Fort I production line. – *B. MacRitchie Collection*

Fort 3572 Fleet 60k at RCAF Station Rockcliffe, Ontario, 1941. – *Jack McNulty Collection*

Fort 3660 without roll bar, prior to delivery to RCAF, at Fort Erie. – *B. MacRitchie Collection*

RCAF 3562 Fleet Fort I at Rockcliffe, Ontario, October 1941, with no fairings over the undercarriage legs. – *Public Archives Canada (PAC) HC11763-3*

Finch, progressing to an intermediate level with the North American Yale, and finally to the North American Harvard. The Fort was to be introduced into the training course as an intermediate trainer. The handling characteristics were good, but an unskilled pilot could get into trouble during steep turns and aerobatics. This may have been due to the ailerons extending to the wing tips, causing early stall of the tips. However, due to reports of poor workmanship and maintenance difficulties, the Fort earned a reputation for poor serviceability that would follow it for the rest of its career. There was one report issued by the RCAF which claimed the first Forts were practically custom-built, and there were over 100 changes to the original design. This made it difficult to determine what spares were required for the aircraft, as many of the components were not interchangeable between the early aircraft.

The RCAF soon found that the Yale was of very little use as a stepping stone to the more powerful Harvard. The use of the intermediate trainer in the instructional process was an unnecessary expense, as it only served to confuse the pupils, especially at the early stages of their flying careers. In fact, it actually slowed down training progress. No difficulty was found in converting pilots from the light aircraft such as the Finch or Tiger Moth, to the North American Harvard advanced trainer. Consequently, the RCAF decided to abandon the program's intermediate trainer step. With this change, and the unsatisfactory experience in the production and maintenance of the Fort aircraft, the original order for Forts was reduced from 200 to 100 aircraft. Thirty-one Forts were delivered in 1941, including the prototype, and the balance of the order (70) was delivered in 1942.

The RCAF now had to decide what to do with the Fort aircraft. It was suggested that the Fort might be suitable as a wireless-operator trainer, since the Menasco-powered Tiger Moths then in use had marginal performance. (The Tiger Moths were never designed to carry such a load of wireless equipment.) It was decided to convert the majority of the Forts to wireless trainers, designated as Fort IIs, with the installation of a T.1083 transmitter and a R.1082 receiver wireless in the rear cockpit replacing the original instructor's control panel. Provision was made for a Radio Direction Finding (RDF) loop on the upper rear fuselage, and an aerial mast was incorporated into the turnover structure (roll-bar) between the two cockpits. The conversion of the Forts was done by Repair Depots at each of the Training Commands. The converted Fort II wireless trainers were issued to No. 3 Wireless School at Winnipeg, with No. 2 Training Command and No. 2 Wireless School at Calgary with No. 4 Training Command.

No. 2 Wireless School was the first to use the Fort in any quantity, with the first aircraft arriving on January 20, 1942. Reports issued by the Wireless Schools did not rate the airplane very highly as a trainer. The plane was still ground-looping due to persistent brake problems. The visibility was poor due to the radial engine and the tail-down flying attitude. Also, the oil system was inadequate and all the engines ran roughly. The relatively high wing loading of the Fort with the wireless aboard (16.9 lbs/sq.ft.) made it difficult for the trainee operators to tune and key the sets in rough weather. Nevertheless, the Forts became the training aircraft for many thousands of wireless operators.

Most pilots found the Fort uninspiring. The late Tommy Williams commented on the difficulty of flying the Fort, but he also said, "I never flew an aircraft in my lifetime that I didn't like after getting to know it well." He felt it was unfair to brand the aircraft with so many disparaging remarks, as he found the Fort a delightful aircraft to fly. We think the truth is somewhere between the two extremes, depending on the pilot's experience and skill.

When more powerful and heavier radio equipment was required such as the T.1154 in the training program, the Forts were phased out and were replaced by Yales and Harvards. The last Forts were withdrawn from service and retired by July 1944.

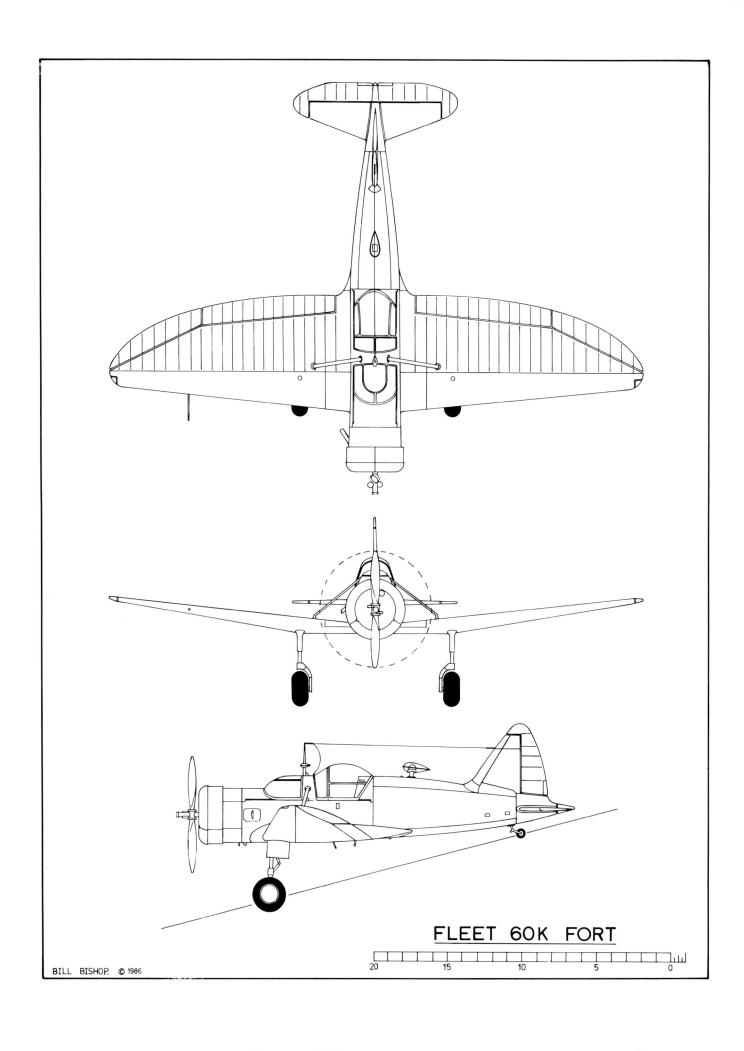

FLEET 60K FORT

20   15   10   5   0

FLEET FORT MODEL 60 DATA

FORT I

Engine:
    330 hp Jacobs L-6MB
Dimensions:
    Wing Span – 36 feet
    Length – 26 feet 10.31 ins.
    Wing Area – 216 sq. ft.
Performance:
    Max. Speed @ sea level – 162 mph
    Cruise Speed @ sea level – 135 mph
    Service Ceiling – 15,000 ft.
    Rate of climb – 1,150 ft/min.
Weights:
    Gross Weight – 3,500 lb.
    Empty Weight – 2,530 lb.

FORT II

Same as Fort I except weight.
Weights:
    Gross Weight – 3,650 lb.
    Empty Weight – 2,601 lb.

A second British mission arrived in late July 1938 as a follow-up to the earlier one. This mission was headed by Sir Hardman Lever. While he stayed in Montreal to talk to Canadian banking interests, a smaller group led by Frederick Handley Page, accompanied by Sir Henry Self, A.C. Boddis and a senior Air Ministry contracts officer, toured the various aircraft manufacturing facilities. They visited Fleet on August 5. On his own initiative, Sanderson had invited two other aircraft industrialists to attend, but they were located too far away to be part of the group. They were Grant MacDonald, Winnipeg, who manufactured floats for bush planes, and Stanley Burke, who headed a small aircraft manufacturing company in Vancouver. Sanderson wanted his two friends there for moral support, when the high-ranking British industrialists paid their official visit to his tiny factory.

After the tours of the aircraft facilities, the various parties sat down at the conference table in Montreal to hammer out a proper agreement to build the Handley Page Hampden bomber (the "Flying Broomstick" or "Pan-Handle"). These meetings lasted for several days and were arduous for everyone concerned. The British members were very anxious to get things rolling, while the Canadians were not organized to handle such a large and complicated project. During the course of the discussion, Jack Sanderson found himself being used as a go-between by the British, because of his straight talk and ability to cut through the various problems, both real and imagined.

An announcement of joint plans was made from Ottawa on September 2, after which the mission left for the U.K. Before leaving, they asked that the Canadian representative come to London so that the contract could be signed. The Canadian delegation, headed by Sanderson, departed for England on September 16, 1938. He left the other manufacturers to form and organize Canadian Associated Aircraft Ltd. (CAA). The six Canadian aircraft companies were to work together to produce the very large Short Stirling bomber, which had not even flown in England, and the Handley Page Hampden medium bomber. The Stirling bomber order was still-born, but the Hampden bomber was eventually built. The CAA was composed of two groups, from Ontario and Quebec companies. Each company would make specific components, and the complete aircraft would be assembled at new facilities at Malton, Ontario, and St. Hubert, Quebec. The project would be financed by the Canadian government. The companies and the components that they manufactured are listed below:

	Ontario	Quebec
Fuselage	Fleet Aircraft Ltd.	Canadian Vickers Ltd.
Wings	Aircraft Div. National Steel Car	Canadian Car & Foundry
Tail	Ottawa Car Manufacturing	Fairchild Aircraft Ltd.

After a meeting at the Air Ministry in London, the Canadians visited the Handley Page factory to see the Hampden being built. In Sanderson's words, "To me, it was not just a case of curiosity, watching the sheets of aluminum being cut into various shapes and sizes, it was fascinating, even frightening. In my thoughts I was trying to visualize our men duplicating each of these operations, and it was obvious that it was going to take a lot of time to become proficient enough to do the precision work that was required. This was due to the different methods used in Europe, [as compared] to those in North America. Also, the English blue-prints used the metric system, while we used inches and our workmen would have to get used to it. [I think Sanderson was referring to the English hardware, bolts and nuts, some of which were close to metric hardware sizes.] Not only that, but we would have to train a lot of new craftsmen to start with, and this would take a lot of time."

The following days spent attending meetings at the Air Ministry were tiresome ones, though to Sanderson they were an education in company formation and business adminstration. During this time he received a telephone call from Air Commodore E.W. Stedman in Ottawa. The Canadian authorities now realized that if the Hampden production went ahead, the Canadian aircraft industry might be unable to honour any contracts placed by the Canadian government. Sanderson was able to reassure Stedman that the Hampden contract would probably enhance the industry's ability to provide aircraft for the Canadian government. On November 16, 1938, the Hampden contract was signed and the Canadians returned home, with exception of Jack Sanderson. He had been asked by Handley Page to discuss their tour of Germany. This tour had been arranged by Hitler, who had invited various foreign indus-trialists and politicians to tour Germany's new industries. From this disquieting discussion, Sanderson became aware of how desperate a situation England found itself in, irrespective of Chamberlain's famous pronouncement of "peace in our time" the previous month. This discussion was to affect Sanderson very deeply and many of his actions and decisions over the next two years would to stem from this experience.

Before leaving for Canada, he arranged for a foreman from each of his departments to visit the Handley Page factory, so that they could get first-hand experience of how the Hampden bomber was built. His last appointment before leaving Britain was a visit to a senior RAF officer at the Air Ministry, where he was recruited to try to sell Canada on the idea a large scale pilot training scheme. The Canadian government had been adamant in its refusal. Now, with war just a few short months away, Britain was desperate.Sanderson was asked to use his best offices when he returned to Canada.

Upon arrival on November 22, 1938, he immediately took a train to Ottawa, where he visited both the Secretary of State and Chief of Air Staff, Air Vice-Marshal G.M. Croil, to whom he presented Britain's case. Though he assisted in drafting a memo on the situation, the best he was able to do in person was to forcefully put forward Britain's desperate case so that when war did break out, Canada would be more receptive to the plan (this eventually became the British Commonwealth Air Training Plan). Sanderson evidently wrote to Mike Pearson, who was working in the High Commissioner's office, at Canada House, London, about this training scheme on December 3, 1938.

Problems had piled up at the Fort Erie plant during his absence. These involved personnel conflicts, trainers being built and overhauled, Freighter assembly, drawings for the Fleet Fort advanced trainers requiring examination and approval, meetings with the contractors in order to get started on new buildings to accommodate the Hampden bomber production.

By the end of 1938 Jack Sanderson found himself appointed as vice-president of the Air Transport Association (CATMAC had shortened its name).

The building of the plant extension had commenced, but nothing had been done to get the blueprints to Canada for the Hampden bomber production by Canadian Associated Aircraft. After checking with his fellow CAA directors and finding they all faced the same situation, he took the matter into his own hands. Without informing his own board of directors, he sailed to England on January 3, 1939, with his purchasing agent, Ab Silcox. On their arrival in England they contacted the person responsible for the U.K. side of the Hampden business. The meeting started very badly when Sanderson was referred to as a "Colonial." Jack fumed and threatened to inform the Air Ministry if the situation did not improve in the next 48 hours. At the same time he got into hot water, as his Fleet board of directors were furious with him for going to England without their permission. They sent him a number of cablegrams, which he ignored. However, a cablegram was also sent to the Canadian High Commissioner in London requesting that the High Commissioner refrain from assisting Jack Sanderson in any way whatsoever while he was in England. Evidently the Canadian government was annoyed at the close ties Sanderson had built up with the British. Fortunately High Commissioner Vincent Massey had a great deal of sympathy for Sanderson's position and what he was attempting to achieve in preparing for the growing conflict.

After resolving the blueprint problem and returning to Canada, he found things at Fleet to be in good shape, thanks to the capable hands of Tom MacCracken, his factory manager. The RCAF was still not showing any interest in the Fleet Fort, though they did request a meeting with him regarding trainers. On arrival in Ottawa, he was told to expect an order for Fleet biplane trainers, which the RCAF estimated could be produced at the rate of $2\frac{1}{2}$ planes a week. They were sceptical when he told them that he could produce at the rate of one a day, but when he revealed that he had been building trainers for just such an order, and that he had fuselage frames hanging from every available rafter in the factory, they were impressed.

Without time to catch his breath, Sanderson had to leave for England again on March 16, 1939, to accompany 19 Fleet Aircraft personnel who were going to spend a couple of months at the Handley Page plant learning how to build the Handley Page Hampden bomber. During his visit to the plant to observe how things were going, he noticed that his men were coming up with ideas on how to make some parts more simply. The exchange was working to the benefit of both parties.

Before returning to Canada he was asked to visit Sir Henry Self, who wanted to discuss a plan similar to that involving the CAA, whereby the Bristol Beaufort would be built by Stanley Burke's company, Boeing of Canada, in Vancouver. Sanderson phoned Burke, who arranged to send his representative to England. Sanderson was expected to wait in England until he arrived. To fill in his time, Sanderson asked if it would be possible to fly a Hampden bomber, and an aircraft powered by a Rolls Royce Merlin engine. Much to his delight, permission was granted, and he spent an enjoyable couple of days flying about the English countryside in a Hampden and a Fairey Battle. Further time was spent playing golf, organized by Mike Pearson, a senior officer in the High Commissioner's office. When the Boeing representative finally arrived they went over the plans together at the Air Ministry. The Boeing man stayed on to examine the Beaufort, while Sanderson returned to Canada. (Unfortunately the original plan was later cancelled by the British, but Boeing did become involved in building the Consolidated Catalina or Canso flying boat.) Sanderson wrote to Mike Pearson at Canada House in April concerning the wind tunnel tests on the new Fort trainer, and the difficult and dirty business of getting orders for trainers.

After his return to Canada, he received a call from a French industrialist in New York, asking for an appointment. Though this incident did not affect the history of Fleet, it is worth recording as part of the history of that time and the state of world affairs. His caller had just returned from Paris, and the interest that he represented had a plan to come to Canada and form a large company to manufacture French planes for the French Air Force. Apparently Sanderson had been recommended to head this Canadian company. Intrigued by the idea, plans were immediately made to sail to France to inspect the French plane and talk to the principals of the organization. Sanderson's words sum up the situation, "To be leaving again on transatlantic crossing, and not staying home to look after the business, it could be said, that I was negligent. The way I looked at it, my factory manager could be classed as one of the best. The directors had installed a comptroller of their own choosing [G.C. Chataway], and that was a good thing as far as I was concerned, as the factory was full of work."

He sailed from New York for England in May 1939, and on arrival boarded one of the large Handley Page Hannibal aircraft to cross the English Channel. There was a lot of frustrating procrastination by the French before Sanderson was shown the aircraft factory which though well equipped, was idle. He finally met with the officials of what is believed to have been part of the Dreyfus group of companies. Sanderson remembers, "When the meetings were finally terminated, I realized that I had been brainwashed, giving them all the knowledge I had obtained from my experiences. All I wanted to do was to get back to London to talk with Handley Page, and then get on a ship for home." He made it back in one piece, but his trip across the Channel in a French airliner ended abruptly after takeoff when there was a loud bang and the aircraft started to shake violently. The pilot turned back to the field and landed between two hangars. On leaving the aircraft Sanderson noted that a bracket supporting the starboard flap had broken.

On July 11, 1939, the RCAF announced that an order had been placed with Fleet Aircraft Ltd. for 27 trainers Model 16 (modified Model 10).This resulted in Fleet placing an order for 36 Kinner engines. The order probably saved Kinner Airplane and Motors Inc. from the final stages of bankruptcy, as the order allowed Earl Herring to reorganize the company as Kinner Motors Inc. in July. The company became a major supplier of engines for the RCAF Finches, and also for the Ryan PT-22 series of trainers for the U.S. Services.

FLEET FINCH MODEL 16

With the changes to the Fleet Model 10, as suggested by the RCAF, Fleet produced a batch of 27 trainers for the Air Force and one additional trainer for Consolidated Aircraft. The RCAF named this Fleet the Finch I or Finch II, depending on the engine type.

The additional trainer that Consolidated asked Fleet to build, was a special Fleet trainer Model 16F or Model 10 in the States. It was also known as a Brewster B-1, as Consolidated had assigned the U.S. rights to the Consolidated Fleet design to the Brewster Aeronautical Corporation, Long Island City. This aircraft was entered in the 1939 competition for a new U.S. Army trainer. Fleet built this one first, even though it was the last of the batch of Model 16s, with a c/n of 262. The Warner Super Scarab engine 175-horsepower was closed cowled similar to the Freighter and Fort. It was registered as NC20699 and later as N2069. It was first flown on February 8, 1939 by Dick Young and later by the Consolidated test pilot George Newman. It was the only Model 16F built. Unfortunately, the competition was won by the Ryan S-T low-wing design. The aircraft still survives today and has recently been presented to the Airpower Museum, Ottumwa, Iowa.

The 27 aircraft manufactured for the RCAF were completed as Fleet Model 16Rs or Finch Is, with 160-horsepower Kinner engines. All 27 were delivered to the Air Force between October 1939 and February 1940. On delivery, most were issued to the Central Flying School at Trenton, Ontario.

There is now some doubt whether Fleet began to manufacture fuselages for the Model 16s in anticipation of further orders as world hostilities intensified. An order for 404 Model 16Bs was finally issued in January 1940. The first Fleet Model 16B, or Finch II, was flown

Canadian built Handley Page Hampden bomber RCAF A386 at Patrica Bay, British Columbia, early 1940s. The fuselages for this plane were built by Fleet. – *Jack McNulty Collection*

Specially built by Fleet in 1939, for Consolidated as Model 16F type or Model 10. This trainer which was entered in the 1939 competition for a new U.S. Army trainer, which was won by the Ryan S-T low wing design. Jack Sanderson (in smock) is standing at the tail. The Fleet Freighter CF-BJT is in the background. – *Ross Zimmerman Collection*

at Fort Erie on March 12, 1940, with Fleet's test pilot Tommy Williams at the controls. The Fleet 16B was equipped with a lower-powered Kinner B-5R of 130-horsepower.

Although Fleet may have stockpiled fuselages and other components in anticipation of orders from the RCAF, production was initially slow. Ironically, production was delayed due to difficulties in obtaining equipment, which was to be supplied by the RCAF. Once this equipment was obtained, the production bottleneck was removed and production accelerated, facilitating a valuable early contribution to the war effort via the pilot training program.

During 1940, 335 Finch IIs were delivered to the RCAF, and 69 were delivered during the first months of 1941. In addition, Fleet delivered ten Model 16Ds or 10Bs to the Portuguese Navy in May 1941. (It is believed that they were ordered as 10Bs but delivered as 16Ds.) In 1942 a further five Model 16Ds were delivered to the Portuguese Navy.

Most of the Finches were used by Elementary Flying Training Schools (EFTS) as part of the British Commonwealth Air Training Plan (BCATP). They continued in use until the summer of 1942 when the Finches were partly replaced by Fairchild Fleet Cornells. The Finch was well liked by the BCATP and served with the following Elementary Flying Training Schools: Nos. 3, 4, 7, 10, 11, 12, 13, 14, 16, 17, 21 and 22. During the summer of 1940 a number of crashes occurred with Finches after they entered inverted spins. Two investigations were held into the crashes, one in Ottawa by Dr. J. Green of the National Research Council at the RCAF Test & Development Establishment, and the other by Fleet.

The investigation held in Ottawa determined that if the height of the rear fuselage fairing was reduced, the aircraft recovered normally. Tommy Williams, using RCAF Finch 4764, felt the trouble had arisen due to the fitting of the two-piece tail-plane, and after the gaps between the fuselage and the tail-plane were taped over, the aircraft recovered normally. Consequently, a metal fairing was fitted to the fuselage on all Model 16s to minimize the gap, and the trouble disappeared.

The last of the Fleet Model 16s remained with the RCAF until 1947, but the great majority of them were struck off strength by October 1944.

FLEET MODEL 16 DATA
(all models except where noted)
FINCH I & II

Engine:
    Model 16B – 130 hp Kinner B5-R, 5 cylinder radial (Finch II)
    Model 16D – 160 hp Kinner B5-2, 5 cylinder radial (Finch I)
    Model 16F – 175 hp Warner Super Scarab, 7 cylinder radial
    Model 16R – 160 hp Kinner R5-2, 5 cylinder radial

Dimensions:
    Wing Span   – 28 ft.
    Length – 21 ft. 8 in. – Model F – 22 ft. 3¼ ins.
    Wing Area   – 194.4 sq. ft.

Rate of climb
    – Model B – 435 ft/min.
    – Model D – 1,000 ft/min.
    – Model F – N/A
    – Model R – 1,000 ft/min.

Performance:
    Max. Speed @ sea level – Model B – 104 mph
        – Model D – 117 mph
        – Model F – 117 mph
        – Model R – 117 mph

Weights:
    Gross Weight
        – Model B – 2,000 lb.
        – Model D – 2,000 lb.
        – Model F – 2,180 lb.
        – Model R – 2,000 lb.

    Cruise Speed @ sea level – Model B – 85 mph
        – Model D – 95 mph
        – Model F – 102 mph
        – Model R – 85 mph

    Empty Weight
        – Model B – 1,122 lb.
        – Model D – 1,148 lb.
        – Model F – 1,342 lb.
        – Model R – 1,148 lb.

    Service ceiling   – Model B – 10,500 ft.
        – Model D – 15,200 ft.
        – Model F – N/A
        – Model R – 15,200 ft.

NOTE: The Model 16D was a Fleet designation, but was changed to Model 16R at the request of the RCAF.

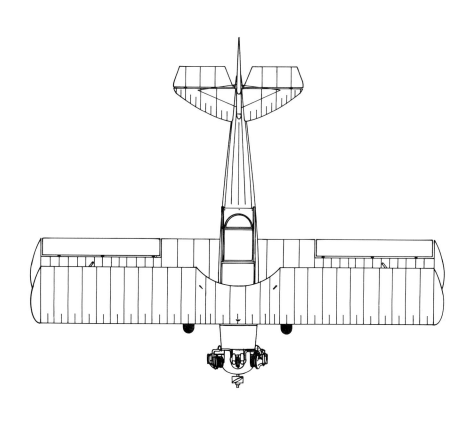

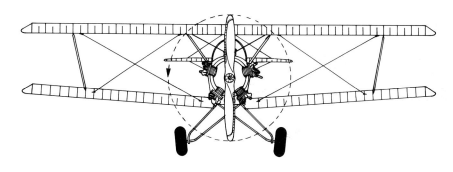

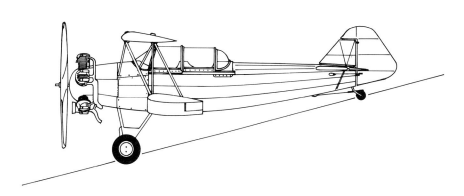

FLEET 16B FINCH

20   15   10   5   0 FEET

A list of all known construction numbers of Model 2/7, 10, and 16, indicating the year and numbers built, are recorded at the end of this chapter (data by Terry Judge).

In 1939, with the world poised on the brink of another great war, Sanderson took stock of his company's position. The number of employees had risen to 400. Trainers were being built for the RCAF, plus a few for export to Portugal and Nicaragua. The Fleet Freighter was still being built, but its reception by the industry was disappointing. Work had begun on building the prototype Fort, even though the RCAF still showed no interest. Work had also begun on building the fuselages for the Hampden bomber, but because of delays and management problems at CAA, it would be another year before the first aircraft would fly. Canada declared war one week after Britain, on September 10, 1939, and Sanderson was called to Ottawa by Robert C.Vaughan not long after declaration. Vaughan, who had been vice-president of Canadian National Railways, was the chairman of the Defence Purchasing Board, which had been formed out under the Defence Purchases, Profits Control, and Financing Act in June 1939. An Aircraft Division was being set up, through which all orders for Canadian-built military aircraft would be placed, including British purchases. Vaughan's call to Sanderson was to invite him to come to Ottawa to take charge of the Aircraft Division. Sanderson's immediate reply was yes, causing his long association with Fleet to be broken for a period of about a year while he performed this hectic duty.

While Sanderson was in Ottawa, a notable thing happened at Fleet in December, it was the building of the water tower at the Fleet factory. This tower became a distinct landmark in the area. It is still there today, 50 years later.

Thus the stage was set for the second decade of Fleet and the significant war years. A listing of the construction numbers c/ns, the year in which they were delivered, their registration and the customer or country of delivery, of all the Fleet trainers and the Freighters are tabulated in the following table.

CANADIAN FLEET AIRCRAFT
MODELS 2/7s, 10, 16, 21, 50 and 60
Construction Number Summary

Year Delivered	c/n	No. of Aircraft	Model No. and Remarks
1930/32	1-10	10	Fleet 2/7s (U.S.-built fuselages)[1]: CF-ANL/ANO, AOC/AOF, ASL, ATO
1931	11-30	20	Fleet 7 Fawn Is for RCAF: 190/209
1931/33	31-32	2	Fleet 7s rebuilt U.S. Fleet 2s: CF-ANH
1935	33-50	18	(Fleet 10s for China/Canton)
1936	51-60	10	Fleet 7C Fawn IIs for RCAF: 213/222
1936	61-68	8	Fleet 7Bs for DND/flying clubs: CF-CEM/CET
1936	69	1	Fleet 7C for UK: G-AEJY
1936	70-76	7	(2 Fleet 10s for Yugoslavia and 5 Fleet 10-32Ds for Mexico: E-2/E-6)
1936	77-80	4	Fleet 7Bs for DND/flying clubs: CF-CFD/CFG
1936	81	1	Fleet ?
1937	82-91	10	Fleet 7C Fawn IIs for RCAF: 228/237
1937	92-97	6	(3 Fleet 10Gs for Portugal: 79/81 3 Fleet 10s for Portugal: 82/84)
1938	98-117	20	Fleet 10As for Argentina: R75/R94
1938	118-124	7	Fleet 7C Fawn IIs for RCAF: 259/265
1938	125	1	Fleet ?
1937	126	1	Fleet 7B for New Zealand: ZK-AGC
1937	127-132	6	(3 Fleet 10Bs and 3 Fleet 10Ds for Venezuela)
1937	1-10	10	10 Fleet 21s to Mexico
1937	1	1	1 Fleet 21 CF-DLC

Year Delivered	c/n	No. of Aircraft	Model No. and Remarks
1938	133	1	(Fleet 10F for Dominican Republic)
1938	134	1	Fleet 10F for Dominican Republic
1938	135-138	4	Fleet 7C Fawn IIs for RCAF: 280/283
1938	139-188	50	Fleet 10B for China
1938	189	1	Fleet 10? (Chinese replacement for c/n 161 sent to Winnipeg F.C.?)
1938	190-199	10	(Unassigned?)
1938/42	200-204	5	Fleet 50 Freighter: CF-BDX
	205-210	6	(Unbuilt Freighters?)
1938	211	1	Fleet 10B for Iraq: YI-SVT
1938	212-240	29	Fleet?[2]
1938	241	1	Fleet 10D for Fleet Aircraft Ltd.
1938	242	1	Fleet ?
1938/39	243-261	19	Fleet 16R Finch Is for RCAF: 1001/1019 (Some c/ns unknown)
1939	262	1	Fleet 16F for Consolidated Aircraft Inc.: NC20699
1939	263	1	Fleet 10F for Nicaragua: GN-14
1939/40	264-690	8	Fleet 16R Finch Is for RCAF: 1020/1027
1940	600	1	Prototype Fleet 60 Fort CF-BQP (RCAF 3540)
1940/41		404	Fleet 16B Finch IIs for RCAF: 4405/4808
1941		10	Fleet 10B for Portugal: 109/118
1941		5	Fleet 16D for Portugal: 131/135
1941	601-627	28	Fleet 60K Fort
1942	628-700	73	Fleet 60K Fort (RCAF 3561-3660)

	No. of Aircraft	Model No. and Remarks
Total	7	Fleet 2s
Total	71	Fleet 7s
Total	122	Fleet 10s
Total	427	Fleet 16s
Total	11	Fleet 21s
Total	5	Fleet 50s
Total	101	Fleet 60s
Grand Total	744	

Author's note: Serial/registration ranges do not necessarily correlate one on one with c/ns range. The only such correlation known is with the RCAF Fawns.

1 Remarks in parentheses are *unconfirmed.*
2 The c/ns 212-261 may have been assigned to the 50 aircraft ordered by China, which was later cancelled.

A frontal view of the special trainer N20699, with belly-tank, at the back of Unit #2. Note the unusual closed-cowled engine. – *Ross Zimmerman Collection*

Fleet Model 16B Finch IIs production line with the lay-out area marked on the floor in the foreground. – *B. MacRitchie Collection*

Complete Fleet Model 16R with canopy RCAF 1006. – *B. MacRitchie Collection*

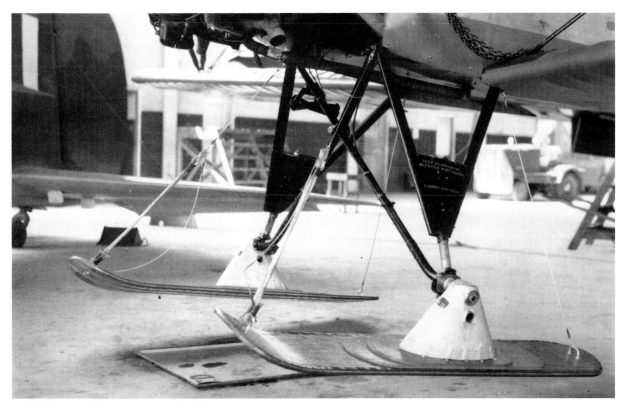

Ski installation on a RCAF Fleet Finch. – *NAM 8613*

Student pilots walking out to their aircraft at No. 4 E.F.T.S. RCAF Windsor Mills, Quebec, July 25, 1940. – *PAC PL-2039*

The first Model 16R delivered to RCAF 1001 restored and registered as CF-AAE, Edmonton Flying Club, at Cold Lake, Alberta, 1977 – *Jack McNulty Collection*

Paul and Joy Soles's restored Fleet Finch II C-FGDM RCAF 4683 – *B. MacRitchie Collection*

Colour
Photos
and
Colour
Profiles
by
Peter Mossman

Fleet 21 over the Niagara area 1984. – *B. MacRitchie Collection*

Fleet Model 2 CF-ANL, in the colours of the Aero Club of B.C.

Fleet Fawn II Model 7C R.C.A.F. 213.

Fleet Model 10 in Portuguese Naval Air Service markings.

Fleet Finch II Model 16B R.C.A.F. 4502.

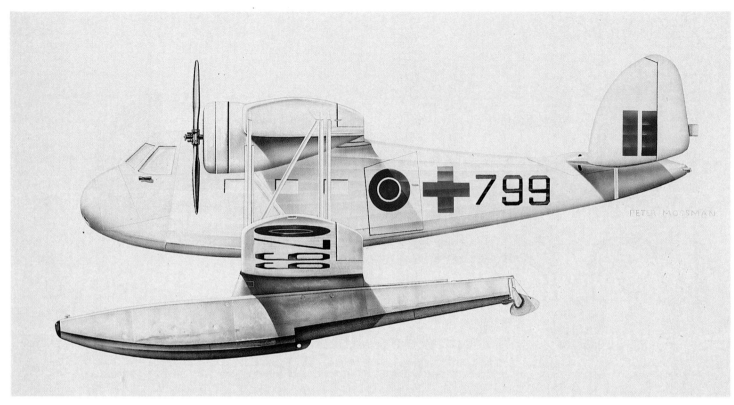

Fleet Freighter Model 50K R.C.A.F. 799 in air ambulance markings.

Fleet Fort II Model 60 R.C.A.F. 3609 wireless trainer.

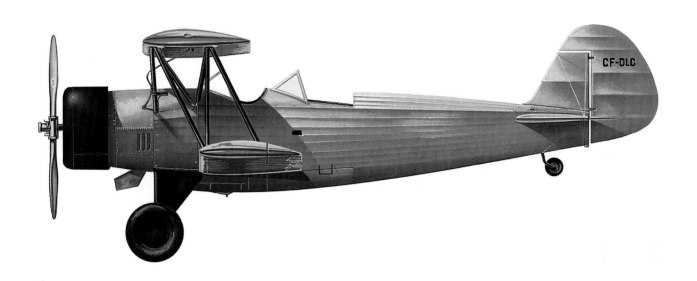

Fleet Model 21M CF-DLC in the original two seater configuration.

Fleet Cornell PT-23 built for the USAAC.

Fleet Cornell PT-26B R.C.A.F. 10835. The 1,000th built and donated to the Air Force by the employees of Fleet. *Spirit of Fleet*.

Fleet Canuck Model 80 CF-EBE of Central Airways Ltd.

Fleet Doman Helicopter CF-IBG-X.

Fleet Helio Courier.

The final product of a lot of work and loving care by the team of the *Spirit of Fleet II* Cornell RCAF 10835, flying near Mount Hope. It is one of the aircraft of Canadian Warplane Heritage Museum collection. Bill Cumming at the controls. – *Gord Hill*

Three Fleets together, Canuck CF-DZM, Fleet Cornell *Spirit of Fleet II* and the Model 21 taking off. – *B. MacRitchie Collection*

A Cornell PT-26 and a PT-23 in flight, showing the different engine installations. – *CWHM*

Cornell PT-23 with the radial engine instead of the in-line Ranger. Fleet built 93 PT-23s for U.S.A.A.C. in 1943. – *Bill Cumming Collection*

Fleet Industries produced for Raytheon the 'Cobra Judy' radar antenna for use by the U.S.Navy. – *Fleet Industries*

Fleet produced 19 fin and rudder sets for the Boeing to be used on 707/E3A aircraft (AWACS).
It was one of the largest aircraft components to be manufactured by Fleet. – *Fleet Industries*

Lockheed honoured Fleet Industries in 1981 for producing the 50th P-3C Orion//CP-140
Aurora flight station cockpit. – *Fleet Industries*

Fleet produced space hardware for Hughes Aircraft, Space and Communication Group, California and also for Spar Aerospace, Toronto for the Canadian Anik C., GOES and GMS satellites. – *Fleet Industries*

The Lockheed Tri-Star wide-body L-1011, for which Fleet manufactured the following components, No. 2 engine nacelle, aft dorsal structure and main landing gear doors.

– Fleet Industries

Fleet Aircraft Limited, London

EMPLOYEE'S CERTIFICATE

NAME ...... R. Zimmerman ......

BADGE NO. ..4153...... DEPT. ...1..A......

DATE EMPLOYED ...Nov. 13/41......

TRADE ......

CATEGORY ......Journeyman......

CHANGE OF CATEGORY ...Group Leader.

DATE OF CHANGE ...Dec. 22/41......

EMPLOYMENT TERMINATED ......

REASON ......

N.T. Sanderson

Personnel Department.

FAL4.8.

Jack Sanderson's brother's signature on Ross Zimmerman's certificate Fleet Aircraft Ltd., London, December 22, 1941.
– *Ross Zimmerman Collection*

Fairey Battle RCAF 1694 in target-tug markings at Toronto Island airport, 1943. Fleet overhauled Battles during the war years. They were sent over from England badly damaged for major overhaul and repair in beautiful packing cases, which were used by some as temporary accommodation. – *Jack McNulty Collection*

IV

THE SECOND DECADE – 1940-49

SANDERSON'S DEFENCE CONTRACT DAYS IN OTTAWA – 1939-1940

Sanderson remained the president and general manager of Fleet while acting as head of the Defence Purchasing Board's Aircraft Division in Ottawa. Both positions were affected by the actions of a country trying to come to terms with a warfooting, and the colossal scale of production that such a stance required.

When Sanderson's appointment was announced on the CBC national news on October 12, it caused a few ripples, as he had not been popular with everyone in government, the Armed Forces and industry. Regardless, he was determined to ride out the storm. He also tried to infect various bureaucrats with some of his own sense of urgency in carrying the war to Germany. His desk quickly filled with piles of contracts, as the Armed Forces had to requisition everything they wanted, from paper clips to battleships, and submit these requisitions to the Defence Purchasing Board.

The American Neutrality Act gave Sanderson trouble, as it prevented the U.S. from supplying material and armaments to any of the belligerents. By late September, with amending provisions ready to be debated, Sanderson made an unofficial visit to Washington to present his views on the Act, as president and general manager of Fleet. Needless to say the embassy in Washington was horrified, as were some of his American friends. Whether his visit had any effect will never be known. "Cash and carry" amendments were signed into law on November 4, 1939. These amendments permitted the warring nations to purchase goods in the U.S.A., but required them to take title to equipment in the States and transport them in their own vessels.

Sanderson's position in Ottawa allowed him to make a powerful contribution to the war effort, even when administration for the ordering of equipment and supplies was reorganized. The Defence Purchasing Board was replaced by the War Supply Board on November 1, 1939. The chairman of this new board was Wallace Campbell, president of Ford Motor Company of Canada, who reported to C.D. Howe, the then Minister of Transport.

There was a rush of orders for aircraft associated with the emerging British Commonwealth Air Training Plan (BCATP), which was announced from Ottawa on December 17, 1939.[1] One of these orders was for the 404 Fleet Finch trainers, but it was not until February 1940 that Fleet finally signed the contract. The production of Fleet and de Havilland Tiger Moth trainers was starting to roll, but the requisition of a twin-engine trainer aircraft presented a problem. Suitable aircraft were essentially non-existent and hundreds were required to train bomber pilots. Fortunately a visit by the president of Cessna, Dwayne Wallace, and his sales manager, with their new twin-engined aircraft, provided a potential solution to this problem. Jack Sanderson knew these men and was only too happy to fly the aircraft and spend the evening with them. He was very impressed with the aircraft and discussed the possibility of using it in the BCATP. However, the financial condition of the Cessna company was not very strong. In fact the company could not finance a large order and a new factory by itself. Nevertheless, with the help of Wallace Campbell in Ottawa and Sir Henry Self's

---

1 The British Commonwealth Air Training Plan is well documented in the book *Aerodrome of Democracy* by F.J. Hatch.

assistant in New York, Sanderson was able to get the Cessna contract approved. Without the contract for the Cessna Crane, as it was to be known in the RCAF, the Cessna company may have folded.

Jack Sanderson gives full credit to the help and coaching he received from R.A.C. Henry while he was in Ottawa. Whether the problem was political, military or industrial, Henry was able to advise Jack or clear the blockage for him.

C.D. Howe was appointed Minister of Munitions and Supply on April 9, 1940. The War Supply Board was dissolved and Wallace Campbell left Ottawa. Howe combed the country for people to man his growing war effort. One of the people he found was Ralph Bell, who was appointed director-general of Aircraft Production on June 19, 1940, and on July 2, was also appointed president of Federal Aircraft Ltd., a Crown corporation set up to handle Avro Anson production.

This Crown corporation was formed to oversee the large number of companies involved with Avro Anson production. The original plan called for Ansons to be supplied from the British production lines for the BCATP. But due to the deteriorating situation in Europe, England was unable to deliver the required aircraft. Therefore the Federal government decided to build the Ansons completely in Canada, and power them with American engines. One of the first bottlenecks the Director of Aircraft Production faced with this program, was the enormous amount of spruce lumber required for the construction of the Anson's wooden wings, and later the all-wooden Avro Anson Mark V. This was settled in a rather stormy meeting with the B.C. Lumber industry executives, at which they finally agreed to co-operate and produce the necessary material.

Another bottleneck was the supply of these engines for the Ansons which were being purchased by the RCAF from an American firm with a subsidiary in Montreal. During the contract meeting with C.D. Howe in New York, Sanderson was able to convince Howe, that from his experience, it was not the right engine. He recommended the use of the Jacobs L-6, which was powering Cessna Bobcat or Crane. This was accepted, Al Jacobs was summoned to New York, and a contract for engines for the Anson II was signed.

By mid-August 1940 Howe had decided to dissolve the executive committee of the Department of Munitions and Supply and to bring in Ralph Bell from Federal Aircraft to take on the full duties as director-general of Aircraft Production. Thus Sanderson found his job had changed, as there was not enough room for both men. He decided to help Bell through his transition, and then handed his resignation to Howe on October 2, 1940.

He was given full credit by Howe for having conceived and brought to fruition the entire Canadian aircraft manufacturing program, which was increasing production daily to meet the demands for aircraft required by the Air Training Plan. Jack Sanderson returned to Fleet company.

THE HECTIC WAR YEARS

In the year that Sanderson was in Ottawa, much had happened at Fleet, and the number of employees had risen from 400 to 1300. The order for 404 Fleet Model 16B trainers early in 1940 was the largest order in Fleet's history to date. Mass production could now start in earnest. The first of these planes flew on March 12, 1940, as a Model 16B registered as RCAF 4405, at the hands of Tommy Williams. The announcement of this order and others was made by the Honourable Rauol Dandurand in the House of Commons on May 21, when it was said that the Fleet trainer order was worth $2,000,000, and that the 40 Hampden fuselages being built for the Canadian Associated Aircraft were worth $1,200,000. Fleet would also overhaul Fairey Battles and Kinner engines, and assemble Avro Ansons.

In May 1940, partly due to worker agitation, the company went from 8¾ hour shifts and a 5½ day week to 10-hour shifts and a six-day week. This was later increased to two ten-hour shifts per day. This increase in working hours allowed Fleet to finish the Finch trainer order ten months ahead of schedule, in March 1941. The construction of the Hampden fuselages was well under way and a further order for 80 aircraft was placed in August 1940. In all, the Ontario Group of the Canadian Associated Aircraft delivered 5 fuselages in 1940, 43 in 1941, and 32 in 1942.

What pleased Sanderson most was that an order had been placed by the RCAF for 200 Fleet Forts and tooling up had started. Fleet recovered the development costs of the prototype, which had been company financed. The prototype had flown on March 22, 1940, and had been evaluated by the RCAF later in May, at Trenton. In addition to the 58 Fairey Battles that were arriving by train flatcars for overhaul, there were a limited number of Avro Ansons arriving for assembly from the British production lines in February 1940. Also there was a constant stream of other aircraft and engines for overhaul and repair.

CENTRAL AIRCRAFT

To relieve the congestion and allow Fleet and other companies to concentrate on production of new aircraft, a new factory was proposed, even before Sanderson left Ottawa. It was to be built at Crumlin near London, Ontario and called Central Aircraft. The ability to do overhaul work on both aircraft and engines, and to make parts for any aircraft as required, would eliminate bottlenecks in production. Sanderson was asked to put this factory in place and hire staff. He found himself forced to divide his time between the Fort Erie plant and the one at Crumlin. When the Central Aircraft factory was completed near the end of 1941, the Fleet senior staff had to be split between Crumlin and Fort Erie.

At the end of 1940 Fleet had to expand to accommodate the amount of work it was receiving, and the company bought the north half of Lot 3 from Orrie L. and Clara E. Storm, on December 12. During the year Walter Deisher had been appointed, general manager, Andy Caygen, manager, and Sid Chiswell, superintendent. Deisher had been associated with Fleet from the early days, and had been their "dollar a year man" in Ottawa for many years, acting as their salesman and assisting with contract negotiations. It was Deisher, who had helped start the Ottawa Flying Club in 1927 and developed the airfield which was later named Uplands and eventually bought by the federal government and further developed as Ottawa International Airport.

Fleet delivered 335 Model 16Rs to the RCAF in September 1940. September was also the month that three employees received their ten year service pins from Fleet. They were Jack Sanderson, A.B. Silcox and Emma Storm who had been Sanderson's secretary since the founding of Fleet Aircraft and was also the company's assistant secretary.

THE END OF THE SANDERSON ERA

In early 1941 the major personnel in the company were as follows

President	W.J. Sanderson
General Manager	Walter N. Deisher
Chief Designer	George E. Otter
Treasurer	G.C. Chataway
Chief Draftsman	John Hawkins
Works Superintendent	S. Chiswell
Purchasing Agent	A.B. Silcox
Personnel Manager	A.G. Mackie

Early in 1941 an event took place which had a major impact on Sanderson's career with Fleet. It was the competition to find an aircraft design to replace the elementary trainers then in use with the BCATP, aircraft such as the Fleet Finch and the de Havilland Tiger Moth.

Invitations were extended to a number of manufacturers and initially five, later seven, aircraft of different types were gathered at Rockcliffe and Trenton for evaluation by the RCAF. The winner of this competition was the Fairchild PT-19 Freshman, later renamed the PT-26 Cornell. In December 1941 the government announced that Fleet would be building the Cornell. It was also announced that the number of different aircraft produced for the BCATP was to be reduced to six, to maximize Canada's production capability. Therefore the Fleet Finch and Hampden work would be wound up and the Fort program, which had been in difficulty, would not be extended. It must have been a hard blow to leave a company that had designed, developed and built a whole range of its own aircraft, then to rejoin his company making planes under licence, and parts for other aircraft manufacturers.

Evidently Jack Sanderson could not live with this way of life. He resigned from Fleet at the board meeting held in Toronto on May 12, 1942. Walter Deisher also resigned as a director with Jack Sanderson but stayed on with the company as general manager during the Cornell production period. Gordon MacMillan was named president. Sanderson's secretary, Emma Storm, resigned two weeks later.

When Sanderson left Fleet, he took a position with Forestry Products Laboratory, a component of Consolidated Waterpower & Paper Co., Wisconsin Rapids, Wisconsin, to develop and produce a plastic material for aircraft use for the U.S. Army Air Corps at Wright Field. This project was successful and the material was used extensively by the Air Corps. In 1944 Jack Sanderson joined the U.S. Government Laboratory at Madison, Wisconsin, as chief of Air Corps Group engaged in carrying out experimental work on behalf of Wright Field. During this period approximately 150 projects were completed. In 1945 he purchased the company that he had built for the Canadian government, Central Aircraft Ltd., London, Ontario. He moved the company into one of the ex-A.O.S. hangars at Malton and changed the name to Sanderson Aircraft Ltd. In the hangar, he manufactured components for de Havillands, operated a Cessna agency, and provided hangar storage and aircraft maintenance. But he was dogged by bad luck and suffered badly from a fire which destroyed the hangar in 1958. He reorganized under the name Sanderson-Acfield Aircraft Ltd. and continued as a Cessna agency. At the age of 65 he did a season of amphibious flying in Newfoundland. After this, in 1967 he moved to British Columbia, where he qualified on helicopters before finally retiring to Victoria, B.C. He died at the age of 85 on January 22, 1984. He was elected posthumously to the Aviation Hall of Fame on April 2, 1984.

FAIRCHILD PT-26A & B and PT-23

CORNELL (nee Freshman)

After a demonstration of the PT-19 and a 165-horsepower Warner Super Scarab-powered civil version, the Fairchild M-62B, the Fairchild PT-19 was selected as the new trainer to replace the aging de Havilland Tiger Moth in the spring of 1941, but the first order was not placed or announced until December, 1941, due to concern about the supply of the Ranger engines for this aircraft.

Fairchild Engine and Airplane Corporation concluded a licensing agreement with the Canadian government, and Fleet Aircraft was chosen as the prime contractor in November 1941. The Canadian Fairchild Aircraft Ltd. at Longueuil, near Montreal, was not consulted, as it was no longer connected with its original American parent company.

As the RAF was also involved in the selection of aircraft for production, both Fleet and Fairchild went to work to design and modify the trainer to suit all customer requirements, which varied slightly for each service, including the U.S. Army Air Corps.

It is significant that PT-19 designer Armand Thieblot designed the wing in such a way that it would start to stall at the wing root and progress out to the tip. This was the opposite behaviour of wings on other aircraft, but it provided aileron control effectiveness throughout

Prototype Fleet built Cornell RCAF 10500 at Cartierville, Quebec, 1947.

– Jack McNulty Collection

RCAF 10738 Cornell, preserved at the National Aviation Museum, Ottawa, Ontario.

– PAC RE 19311-1

the early stages of the stall, allowing the student pilot ample time to recover before entering a spin.

The aircraft was to be used by the RCAF up to the basic stage of flight training. It would be powered by the large 200-horsepower Ranger engine and equipped with a generator, battery, blind flying hood, instruments, lights, heater and sliding hood. The name Freshman was selected for the new trainer, but in 1942 it was renamed the Cornell.

Originally developed by Fairchild Aircraft as the M-62 in 1940, the Cornell was built in large quantities. The low-wing monoplane received the U.S. military designation PT-19, with over 4,800 PT-19As and PT-19Bs being built by Fairchild, Aeronca and the St. Louis Airplane Company. The PT-19 was built with an open cockpit and powered with the 175 hp in-line six cylinder inverted Ranger engine. It was used as a primary flight and instrument trainer.

As a possible safeguard against a shortage of Ranger engines, alternative engines were considered, among them the 175-horsepower Warner Scarab, 240-horsepower Continental W-670MA, and the 225-horsepower Jacobs L4MB. A version of the PT-19 with the 220-horsepower Continental R-670-11 was produced for the USAAC. This version did not appeal to the RCAF, as the Continental engine was heavier than the Ranger and would reduce the stress reserve margin. Fairchild was requested to investigate the design of a 205-horsepower D.H. Gipsy Six II installation, but was shortly advised that the engine would not be available from England. The RCAF asked Fairchild to proceed with a design for the 190 horsepower Lycoming O-435-9 installation.

Assigned U.S. military designation PT-26, the aircraft was produced in various forms for the respective services. Fairchild Aircraft in the United States produced the PT-26 Cornell I to RAF specifications under the lend-lease program. In Canada, Fleet aircraft built the PT-26A Cornell II and PT-26B Cornell III to suit RAF and RCAF specifications respectively.

There were slight variations in the three versions. The PT-26 had a Tuf-on plastic finish on the wings, larger rudder, wind-driven generator, hand starter, wooden flaps, no identification lights, oil dilution system, Sensenich propeller, U.S.-type instruments, navigation lights on the wing leading edge, and rudder trailing edge with night roundels. The PT-26A version had a madapollam covering on the wing, smaller rudder than the PT-26, engine-driven generator, electric starter, metal flaps, no identification lights, oil dilution system, S & S propeller, U.S. and Canadian instruments, navigation lights on the wingtips and top of the rudder, and night roundels. The PT-26B was similar to the PT-26A except it had upward and downward identification lights, no oil dilution system, Canadian instruments, and day roundels.

All Cornells had steel-tube fuselages with fabric covering. The wing was manufactured in three sections with a wooden spruce spar and rib structure. The ribs were of the Warren truss type with spruce cap strips and bracing. It was mahogany plywood covered, as were the horizontal and vertical stabilizers. All the control surfaces were fabric covered over a metal structure. The undercarriage was non-retractable.

The first ten Fleet-built Cornells incorporated many Fairchild-built components. The prototype Fleet-built Cornell, RCAF 10500, a PT-26B, was first flown on July 9, 1942, at Fort Erie by Tommy Williams, after testing the last of the Fleet Fort production.

Fleet used sub-contractors in building the Cornell. One of their principal sub-contractors was Dominion Electrohome Industries Ltd., Kitchener, Ontario which produced wings, centre sections, seats, stabilizers and tail fins. Electrohome woodworking division was treated by Fleet as if was one its own, because such good working relationship existed between them.

Fleet Cornell PT-26B RCAF 10711 at Toronto Island Airport, 1943. – *Jack McNulty Collection*

Two Fleet Cornells on skis of 'Little Norway II' training centre of the Royal Norwegian Air Force. Aircraft 173 named 'Sweden I' and 189 'Illinois' in flight near Gravenhurst, Ontario, March 1943. – *PAC 115427*

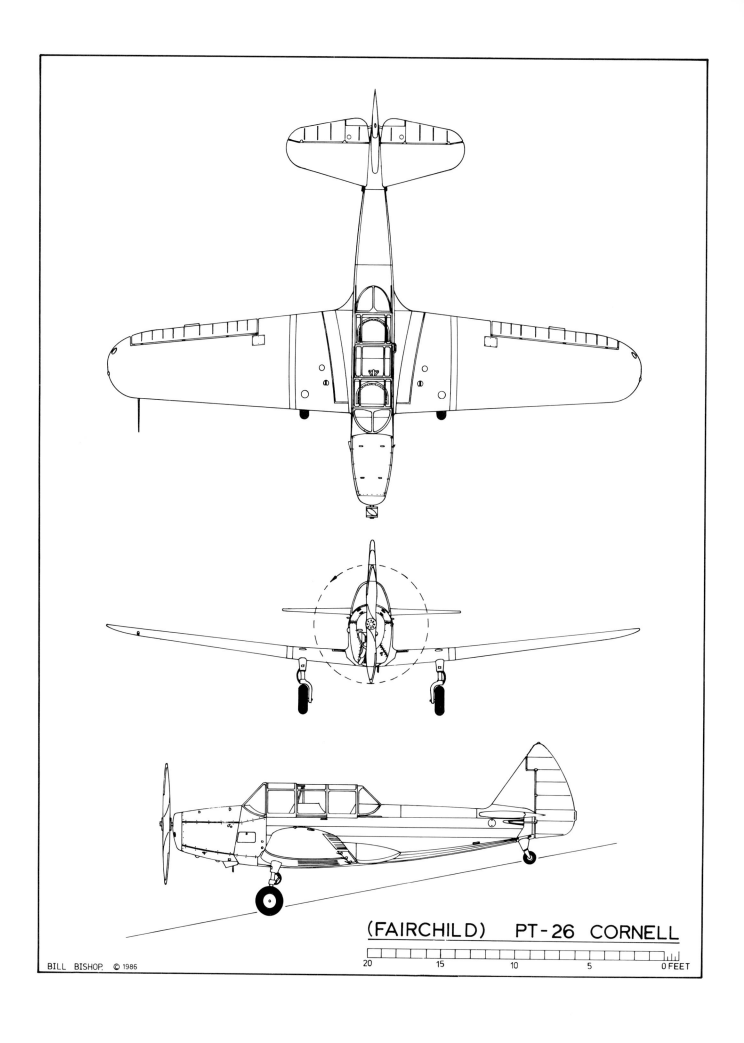

(FAIRCHILD) PT-26 CORNELL

20   15   10   5   0 FEET

The third Cornell built in Canada, 10502, was sent to Central Aircraft at London, Ontario, for installation of a Lycoming engine. The installation was completed by February 1943, and the Lycoming-powered Cornell was first flown on March 13, 1943, by Robert Wingfield. Testing was done at the RCAF's Test & Development Establishment in August 1943. The Lycoming-powered Cornell performed well, attaining a maximum speed of 119.4 miles per hour, an initial rate of climb of 740 feet per minute and a service ceiling of 17,000 feet at a loaded weight of 2,650 pounds. As the supply of Ranger engines was maintained, the Lycoming-powered Cornell was never placed into production. It was eventually converted back to a Ranger engined Cornell.

An order for 93 Continental-powered PT-23s was received from the USAAC early in 1942. The Canadian-built PT-23 was identical to the U.S.-built aircraft except that the Canadian version may have had metal flaps and madapollam-covered wings similar to the PT-26A & Bs. The first Canadian-built PT-23 was flown at Fort Erie by Tommy Williams on November 23, 1942. Six PT-23s were delivered to the USAAC by the end of 1942, the balance of the order, 87 aircraft, was completed by April 1943. The promised order of 600 PT-23s for the USAAC did not materialize and the PT-23 program was terminated once the initial order was completed.

The USAAC did place orders for PT-26s to be built by Fleet Aircraft. The majority went to the RAF under lend-lease and 290 were given to Canada in exchange for 286 Boeing PT-27 Stearman or Kaydets, which were returned to the United States by the RCAF.

The Cornell program called for a target of 150 aircraft to be produced per month by July 1943, but this production rate was not reached until the last quarter of 1943, with deliveries of 140, 150 and 161 aircraft being recorded for October, November and December respectively. By December, 2,100 Cornells had been ordered. The program was reviewed at this time and Fleet was ordered to cut back production to 50 per month. The Cornell program was terminated in June 1944, with the result that only 1,809 PT-26As & Bs had been produced plus the 93 PT-23s, making a total of 1,902 including all models. Bill Cumming has spent many hours researching the production records and archives to arrive at this total of Fleet-built Cornells (see Table I for details).

RCAF Cornells replaced the DH-82C Tiger Moths and Fleet 16B Finches at Elementary Flying Training Schools of the BCATP. RAF Cornells were also used in training schools in South Africa and India.

The Cornell usually operated on wheels, but the Alberta Motor Boat Company built skis for the Cornell using an RCAF design. The skis were installed on Cornells used by some of the Elementary Training Schools, ie. No. 11 EFTS at Cap de la Madeleine, Quebec, as well as by the Royal Norwegian Air Force, who trained on the aircraft at Little Norway in the Muskokas during WW II.

At some high-altitude training schools, like that of High River, Alberta, the Cornell's performance left a lot to be desired. On warm days its performance was inadequate, with long takeoff runs and slow climb rates. During 1943 a series of wing structural failures occurred, which necessitated a reinforcement of the centre-section main-spar to correct the problem. But in general, the Cornells were well liked and did not retire from the RCAF until 1948, when they were replaced by the Canadian de Havilland Chipmunk.

CORNELL DATA

Engine:
PT – 23	– 220 hp Continental W-670-11, 9 cylinder radial
PT – 26A/B	– 200 hp Ranger 6-440-C5, 6 cylinder inline, inverted

Dimensions:
Wing Span	– 36 ft. 11³⁄₁₆ in.
Length	– PT-23 – 25 ft. 10⅞ in.
	– PT-26A/B – 28 ft. 8 in.
Wing Area	– 200 sq. ft.

Performance:
Max. Speed @ sea level	– PT-23 – 131 mph
	– PT-26A/B – 122 mph
Cruise Speed @ sea level	– PT-23 – 109 mph
	– PT-26A/B – 101 mph
Service Ceiling	– PT-23 – 13,000 ft.
	– PT-26A/B – 13,200 ft.
Rate of Climb	– PT-23 – 655 ft/min.
	– PT-26A/B – 645 ft/min.

Weights:
Gross Weight	– PT-23 – 2,900 lb.
	– PT-26A/B – 2,800 lb.
Empty Weight	– PT-23 – 2,046 lb.
	– PT-26A/B – 2,022 lb.

The 1941 Cornell contract was a major challenge for Fleet, requiring massive expansion in all areas, as well as increased production and provision for overhaul mentioned previously, 58 Fairey Battles were overhauled in the period 1941-42. They arrived on railway flatcars and were in various states of damage from flying accidents and enemy action.

To accommodate the expansion, on October 21, 1941, more land was bought from Mr. and Mrs. W.D. Ferguson. This land consisted of the south half of Lot 4.

On January 29, 1942, the first copy of the company's news letter *Plane Talk*, was issued. It was originated by Ray Hubbel and Lew Broach, and became a popular item. It was also a good reference in trying to reconstruct Fleet's history.

On July 2, 1942, Ralph Miliani joined Fleet as test pilot, sharing the load with Tommy Williams. Unfortunately, Miliani was later killed in a tragic mid-air collision with a U.S. Aircobra while testing a Cornell.

The first Fleet Cornell was accepted by the RCAF on July 22, 1942. Fleet's amazing feat of production conversion was accomplished in less than eight months.

Fleet demonstrated a remarkable increase in productivity on the Cornell by decreasing the man-hours per pound of aircraft from 7.66 to 1.91, at an average cost of 63.4 cents per hour of production. The average cost of an aircraft was then $1,338. From 1942 to 1944 a total of 1,902 Cornells were produced for the RCAF and RAF, and 93 Fairchild PT-23s for the USAAC. The total value of the Cornell contract, including spares, tooling and subcontractors, was valued at $23,547,491.

The peak production period was in the last quarter of 1943, when 451 aircraft were completed, achieving a production rate per month of 161 versus a maximum scheduled 150 aircraft in December 1943. The 1,000th Cornell aircraft was produced on October 21, 1943. This aircraft was donated by the employees, as their contribution to the war effort. It was christened by Mrs. M. Mark as *The Spirit of Fleet*. This aircraft represented the 1,942nd aircraft built by Fleet since 1930 and its 1,638th aircraft delivered since the war began, a remarkable achievement. A follow-up order for a further 600 aircraft was never authorized as the Air Training Plan had produced an overabundance of aircrew[2]. On April 6, 1943 during

---

2 One of the authors can testify to this, as he joined the RAF via the Oxford University Air Squadron in 1943 and did not obtain his wings until early 1945.

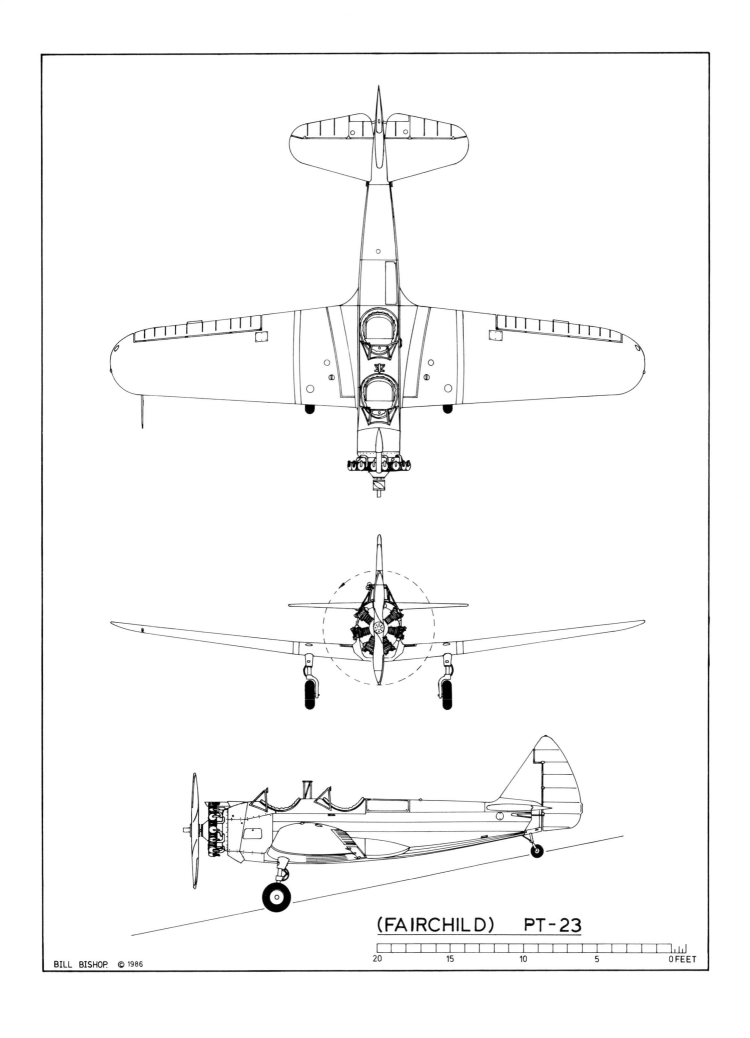

(FAIRCHILD)   PT-23

20   15   10   5   0 FEET

BILL BISHOP. © 1986

Fleet plant with over 50 Fleet Fairchild Cornells lined up outside, taken from a Cornell piloted by Tommy Williams, January 7, 1944. – *B. MacRitchie Collection*

Walter Diesher, Fleet general manager, handing over the 1000th Cornell donated by the Fleet employees as their donation to the war effort to Air Vice Marshal Breadner with Gibb Mackie looking on. It was named the *Spirit of Fleet*. Note the union symbol on the fuselage above A/V/M's shoulder. – *B. MacRitchie Collection*

The Spirit of Fleet flying over the Fleet plant with Tommy Williams at the controls, October 1943. – *B. MacRitchie Collection*

FLEET AIRCRAFT
LIMITED

Plane Talk

Vol. 3, Edition 4   FORT ERIE, ONTARIO   April 10, 1944

FAL PHOTO 168.132

Eleven are Home   •   *"Put Victory First"*   •   *Problem No. 1*

Fleet Cornell RCAF 14437, California December 18, 1946. – *Jack McNulty Collection Collection*

Postwar Cornell in the service of the RCMP Air Division CF-MPK at Mount Hope, Ontario, July 1956. – *Jack McNulty Collection*

this high-productivity period, the company decided to cancel the stock options of all the employees, retroactive to December 1, 1942.

During 1943 the Canadian Associate Aircraft organization was wound up and disbanded.

By the end of that year Fleet's number of employees had reached 2,800, quite a leap from the early days in the 30s.

SUMMARY OF FLEET-BUILT CORNELLS

CONS DESIG	USAAC DESIG	C/N	NAME	RAF SERIAL	RCAF SERIAL	NO. BUILT	AIR FORCE
M62A-3	PT-26A-FE	T4-4670 to -4999	Cornell II	FV100-429	15001-15330	330	RCAF/RAF
M62A-3	PT-26A-FE	T4-6000 to -6068	Cornell II	FV430-516	15331-15417	87	RCAF/ RNoAF RAF
M-62A3		884-1267	Cornell II	FV517-899		384	RCAF/RAF
	PT-26A-FE	T4?	Cornell II	FT542-831	14381-14670	290	RCAF
	PT-26A-FE	T4?	Cornell II	FW881-980		100	RAF
M-62A3			Cornell II	FW981-999		19	RAF
M-62A3			Cornell II	FW100-197		98	RAF/RCAF
M-62A3		FC1-251	Cornell II		10500-10750	251	RCAF
	PT-26B-FE		Cornell II	FZ198-354	10751-10907	157	RNoAF/ RCAF
	PT-26B-FE		Cornell II	FZ355-427		73	RAF
	PT-26B-FE		Cornell II	FZ699-718		20	RAF
	PT-23-FE	FE-1 to -93				93	USAAC
Total Cornells Built by Fleet						1,902	

NOTES;

1. Not all Fleet-Cornells were assigned a construction number. Those particular airframes used RAF serial numbers as their construction numbers.

2. Cornells 14381-14670 were purchased by the USAAC and given to RCAF in exchange for 286 PT-27 Stearmans which were later returned to the United States.

3. All PT-26Bs were procured under the lend-lease program and paid for by the U.S. Army.

4. All PT-26As in the FV series were purchased under the lend-lease program.

5. The PT-26Bs have been called Cornell IIIs in some references, but this terminology was never formally adopted by the RAF/RCAF.

Bill Cumming
January 10, 1989

AVRO LANCASTER OUTER WINGS, TRAILING EDGES & ELEVATORS

In the spring of 1944 Fleet Aircraft was asked by the government to wind down the Cornell production contract with minimum labour disruption and to concentrate on a subcontract for Victory Aircraft Ltd. at Malton, making the famous Avro Lancaster bomber outer wing sets. Victory Aircraft was to become Avro Canada Ltd. after the war. McDonnell Douglas Canada now uses these original facilities at Malton.

This particular contract was for 200 Lancaster outer wings and elevators, plus two sets for the Avro Lincoln bomber, which was to be produced to replace the Lancaster at the end of the war. It is interesting to note, from the late Fred Smye's records of his involvement in wartime aircraft production, that production of the Avro Lancaster bomber in Canada was discussed at a meeting in Washington, on September 18, 1941, at the offices of the British Supply Council. Present at the meeting were Mr. E.P. Taylor (chairman), Sir Henry Self, Hon. C.D. Howe, Air Marshal Harris, Air Vice-Marshal Stedman, Mr. C.R. Fairey, Mr. Ralph P. Bell, Mr. J.B. Carswell, Mr. F. Smye and Mr. Leslie Chance (secretary). The minutes of the meeting record the following discussion:

Mr. Taylor said that on his recent visit to England, the Minister of Aircraft Production had stressed to him the importance which the Home Government attached to production in Canada of heavy bombers of the British type (Lancaster). Mr. Howe said that the Canadians would be glad to undertake the production of heavy bombers provided that the requirements of the Royal Canadian Air Force for 218 medium bombers (Hampden) could be protected. He pointed out that Canadians had undertaken production in Canada of these machines and hoped for deliveries beginning in August 1942, which would give a total of 75 machines in that year and 25 a month thereafter.

After discussion it was finally agreed that Canadians would undertake production of the Lancaster-type heavy bomber in Canada, subject to the following conditions:

a) that provisions be made for the requirements of the RCAF for 218 medium bombers from the U.S. production at approximately the same rate as set out above for the proposed Canadian production. The type of machine which would be acceptable to the RCAF would be agreed between Air Vice-Marshal Stedman and the British Air Commission. The dollar value of deliveries to Canada of medium bombers from U.S. production would be offset against the dollar value of Canadian production of Lancasters.

b) that the necessary negotiations with the U.S. for the transfer to Canada under the terms of the Lend-Lease Act of the 218 medium bombers referred to above would be undertaken by the U.K.

c) that the initial order placed with Canada for Lancaster aircraft should be for not less than 250 machines.

d) that the U.K. would undertake the necessary negotiations for the supply of suitable engines for installation in the Lancaster airframes agreed to be produced in Canada as above.

e) that the U.K. agree to supply to Canada 240 Merlins from the Packard production for installation in the Hurricane aircraft being produced in Canada and intended for delivery to the Chinese Republic (an interesting record of history in the making).

This type of work, in contracting to make aircraft parts was to become Fleet's future role in the aircraft industry and was the beginning of the end of production of their own complete aircraft.

Again, with the enthusiasm of the Cornell contract, Fleet tooled up and produced the wing sets in less than half the time originally agreed upon, 15 versus 36 months, at one third of the cost in man-hours originally estimated, 800 versus 2,400 hours per set. This is dramatically illustrated in the following table:

Production Labour Costs Improvement for Lancaster Wings

Quantity Order	Ordered Cumulative	Average Labour Hours Per A/C Set	Per Pound
5	5	11.535	5.41
10	15	8.673	4.27
4	19	8.193	3.39
20	39	6.475	3.04
20	59	4.915	2.31

Cornell 10511 underneath a Lancaster bomber. Fleet manufactured the outer-wings of the Lancaster for Victory Aircraft at Malton, Ontario. – *NAM 16274*

Canadian Avro Lancaster bombers lined up ready to be ferried to England. – *NAM 16274*

20	79	4.507	2.11
20	99	4.396	2.06
20	119	4.238	1.99
25	144	3.987	1.87
25	169	3.842	1.80
25	194	3.634	1.71
25	219	3.218	1.51
25	244	3.336	1.56
25	269	3.215	1.51
25	294	3.273	1.54
5	299	3.423	1.61

Initially Fleet produced wing-kit parts (43) for Victory Aircraft Ltd. and later manufactured the total components and assembled the wings (the initial 10 wing-sets were produced using some Victory Aircraft components). The first complete Fleet-manufactured wings were produced in July 1944. The production record is illustrated in the table below:

Production of LANCASTER OuterWing and Elevators at Fleet

	1944	1945	Total
Kits of Wing Parts	43	-	43
Complete Wing – Assembly	10	-	10
– Complete	116.5	182.5	299
Trailing Edge – Assembly	10	-	10
– Complete	148	201	349
Elevators – Assembly	20	-	20
– Complete	155	137	292

Note: Fleet produced approximately 50% of the outer-wing production for the 430 Lancasters built by Victory Aircraft Ltd.

It should be recorded that Fleet Aircraft produced the greatest number of aircraft per employee of any aircraft company in North America during the hectic war years.

To help maintain the spirit of the war effort at Fleet, a Lancaster bomber landed at the Fort Erie strip on March 6, 1944. This was the largest aircraft to land on the limited 2,400 foot runway at Fleet. Many of employees were allowed to view the aircraft at close-hand during its visit.

As 1945 progressed, the end of the European war was in sight and discussions commenced regarding what the company should do with its expanded production capability. One of the suggested programs was the building of a light civil aircraft for private and flying clubs across Canada. The company wrote a specification of their requirements and found that the aircraft that best suited their specifications was one built and designed by Noury Aircraft Ltd.

FLEET CANUCK MODEL 80

The beginnings of the Fleet Model 80 Canuck go back to 1939, when J. Omer (Bob) Noury, an air engineer with the Ottawa Flying Club, decided to design and build a light aircraft for the Canadian market. The aircraft was a high-wing monoplane of conventional structure using a welded steel-tube fuselage and tail surfaces, and powered with a 65-horse-power Continental flat four-cylinder engine. The Noury T-65 Series 1 design was first flown on January 21, 1940. The aircraft was given a certificate of airworthiness and Noury sold it in 1941. Bob Noury became a well-known aircraft subcontractor during the war years.

In 1942 he formed Noury Aircraft Ltd. at Stoney Creek, with himself as president and general manager. His intent was to design and build a light aircraft based on his own monoplane design. The Noury N-75 featured side-by-side seating and a 75-horsepower Continental engine. It was test flown from the Hamilton Airport at Mount Hope late in 1944 by T. Borden Fawcett, Noury's test pilot and sales manager. Noury also designed and built a tandem-seat version with a slightly reduced wing span. It first flew on November 24, 1945, from Hamilton Airport with Fawcett at the controls. Noury built three aircraft before selling the rights to Fleet.

Fleet Aircraft felt that the side-by-side design aircraft met most of their specifications, so in May 1945 they purchased the prototype and design rights for this plane from Noury Aircraft.

The Noury was shipped to Fleet's facilities at Fort Erie and was test flown by Fleet's test pilot, Tommy Williams, on June 4, 1945. Williams reported that the original fin design was too small and set to starboard instead of to port. This deficiency necessitated full right rudder to control the aircraft. Test-flying continued until July 26, when the aircraft was put into the shop for modifications to meet Fleet's specifications.

The principal modifications were to the forward fuselage geometry, lowering the engine four inches to improve the forward visibility, and moving the engine forward four inches to allow the relocation of the fuel tank from the centre section of the wing to the forward fuselage. This made possible the installation of a clear skylight in the cabin roof. The original Continental C-75 engine was replaced by a more powerful Model C-85, and a new fin and rudder were installed.

The redesigned aircraft emerged from Fleet's shops as the Model 80 and was named the Canuck. Fleet's vice-president and general manager, Walter Deisher reportedly named the plane in honour of the Curtiss JN-4 (Canadian) he flew at Ottawa after the First World War. The Canuck was first flown in its modified form on September 26, 1945. Tooling and jigs were then set up to produce the Canuck in quantity, and Fleet was back in the aircraft manufacturing business.

Fleet's wartime experience with wooden aircraft had proved conclusively that wood is definitely unreliable as a structural material. The Canuck's fuselage was constructed of welded steel tube and fabric covered. The wings for all production Canucks had extruded Duralumin spars, sheet Duralumin ribs and were fabric covered.

The first intention was to offer the Canuck in two versions, tandem and side-by-side. After discussions with interested parties, it became apparent that the tandem seating in this type of aircraft was a thing of the past for both private flying and civilian instruction purposes. Therefore, all effort was concentrated on the side-by-side version.

Dual controls with conventional sticks were considered a necessity for the Canuck, and the instrument panel was simple and spartan, in keeping with the philosophy of the design. Hydraulic brakes and full-swivelling steerable tail-wheel were provided to give the Canuck good ground-handling qualities.

The 85-horsepower Continental engine with its fuel injection system proved to be a popular feature. When the Canuck was first introduced, it was announced that other engines would be optional, but this was never followed up. The Canuck was offered at a selling price of $3,869.25 plus $247.63 tax.

The Canuck proved to be a very versatile type of aircraft being certified on wheels, skis, and floats. The floats for the Canuck were designed and tested during June 1946. The Fleet designs of the ski and float installations were noteworthy for their simplicity, as the skis and floats could be attached directly to the normal landing gear. This made the change-

Prototype Fleet Model 80 Canuck CF-BYW-X, 1945, a little worse for wear. This aircraft is now in the Harry Whereatt collection at Assiniboine, Manitoba. – *B. MacRitchie Collection*

Standard production Fleet Canuck of Central Airways which used it for flight training at Toronto Island Airport. This aircraft CF-EBE (c/n 149) is part of the National Aviation Museum, Ottawa, Ontario. – *NAM 11886*

over from wheels to skis or floats comparatively easy and straightforward. Canucks were also capable of aerobatic performance, as the design was stressed to the British requirements, with a minimum load factor of 7G.

Fleet obtained certification from the Department of Transport once the development and design were completed. Production rose to four aircraft per day. Standard Canucks were finished in combinations of RCAF yellow and Consolidated blue. The expected sales were slow in coming, and according to one company executive, "Planes were soon stacked about the plant on their engine mounts like dominoes." It was a sturdy aircraft, he noted.

A single three-seat Canuck was made, in which the third person was accommodated on a jump seat in the baggage compartment. This design was designated the Model 81 and was produced in 1947 and registered as CF-FAL. It is still on the registry today (registered to a Prince Edward Island resident) but it was converted back to a Model 80 before being sold to the private market.

Between 1945 and 1948, 198 Canuck aircraft were built by Fleet. The Canuck proved popular and initially sold well to flying clubs, charter companies and private owners in Canada. In addition 24 were exported: 19 to Argentina, 3 to Brazil and 1 each to Portugal and the United States. By late 1947, plagued by postwar financial difficulties and the sales slowdown that affected all aircraft manufacturers, Fleet was forced to terminate production of the Canuck model. To raise necessary cash to keep the company going, all the jigs, tools and completed components were sold to Leavens Brothers Ltd. of Toronto. Leavens continued to assemble Canucks by special order until 1958, when the last steel-tube fuselage was used. The earlier assembled aircraft used mostly Fleet-built components, but later aircraft required more and more manufacturing of parts as the stock of Fleet-built parts was used up. Leavens Bros. assembled 25 aircraft and one additional aircraft was assembled by the St. Catharines Flying Club, using a production airframe and spare components. Total number of Canucks built was 225, including the Noury prototype.

The remaining parts and drawings were sold to Marcel Dorion Aviation of Montreal. This company intended to develop the design into a four-seater aircraft, but this plane was never completed.

The Canucks proved durable and popular with the flying clubs and schools. In 1980, 95 Canucks were still on the Canadian Civil Aircraft Register, with others still flying in the United States and Argentina. The fact that such a large number survived to that date attests to their ruggedness, like the earlier Fleet models Fawn and Finch. Thousands of Canadian pilots learned to fly on the Canuck during the 50s and 60s, and into the 70s. A few are still playing this role even today (as mentioned by Bruce MacRitchie in his foreword).

CANUCK MODEL 80 DATA

Engine:
85 hp Continental C85-12J

Dimensions:

Wing Span	– 34 ft.		
Length	– 22 ft. 4.5 in.		
Wing Area	– 173.5 sq. ft.		

Weights:	Wheels	Skis	Floats
Empty Weight	– 934 lb.	989 lb.	1077.5 lb.
Gross Weight	– 1,480 lb.	1525 lb.	1525 lb.

Performance:

	Wheels	Skis	Floats
Max. Speed	– 111.5 mph	105.5 mph	103 mph
Cruise Speed	– 93 mph	90 mph	85 mph
Service Ceiling	– 12,000 ft.	11,200 ft.	10,000 ft.
Rate of Climb	– 550 ft/min.	475 ft/min.	425 ft/min.

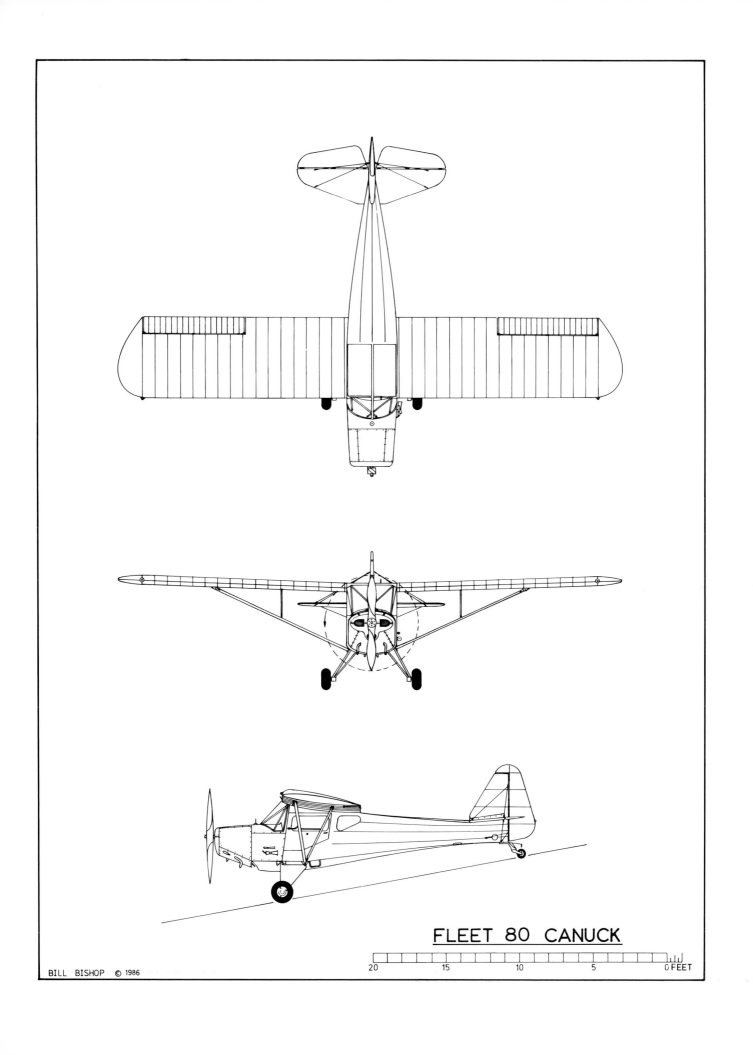

FLEET 80 CANUCK

20   15   10   5   0 FEET

The original installation of the Fleet floats on the Fleet Canuck CF-DEE on the Niagara River, with spreader bars. Note the added ventral fin and dual water rudders added for better control on floats. – *NAM 14450*

The later float installation using Fleet Model 1515 floats on the Fleet 80 Canuck CF-DPY. In this case the normal undercarriage was used as part of the float attachment, without spreader bars. – *NAM 14448*

The Fleet 81 Canuck, the only three seater built CF-FAL (c/n X-238), Mount Hope, Ontario, July 1952. – *Jack McNulty Collection*

A close-up of the Fleet Canuck ski installation, designed and built by Fleet, Charlottetown, Prince Edward Island, March 1947. – *NAM 5717*

The CabinCar and the Fleet 80 Canuck, the two postwar products of Fleet Manufacturing Ltd. with unidentified management in front. – *B. MacRitchie Collection*

V

THE TURBULENT POSTWAR YEARS 1945-1949

Like many other manufacturing companies in Canada, Fleet had to grapple with the return to peace in 1945 and the consequent cancellation of major government contracts. Fleet hoped to employ its large work force and its facilities in the production of the Canuck, but that project was not enough to sustain such a large company.

On July 4, 1946, the Vincent Group bought out the shareholders of Fleet and Norman Vincent became president. The company was renamed Fleet Manufacturing & Aircraft Ltd. to reflect its new versatility. In October 1946 Norman Vincent offered a share exchange, but Fleet directors resigned in protest. In December of the same year the company was acquired by a new group headed by Harrison Securities Corporation, Toronto, with Vincent remaining as president and T.R.Harrison as vice-president. The new management tried to find products other than aircraft that Fleet could mass produce.

FLEET CABINCAR TRAILERS

In 1947 the company produced Fleet CabinCar Trailers for the postwar market. This trailer was meant to provide housing and to facilitate vacation travel. The CabinCar, a low-priced, lightweight, roomy cabin trailer, would be produced in Canada by Vincent Mining Corp. Ltd. In addition to the Canadian market, the Corporation hoped to export the new rolling home to the States in large quantities. The initial production target was for 10,000 units, but when Vincent received the optimistic promise of large American orders, it was increased to 50,000 units, worth $25,000,000. Fleet was contracted to produce the CabinCar on a large-scale, mass-production basis, if the present Fleet shareholders would convert their shares at the rate of one for two in a new Fleet company incorporated in the United States. (It is presumed that this was the exchange of shares that was referred to earlier and resulted in the resignation of the Fleet board.) Tony Smith was named general manager of the new company. The CabinCar was designed by J.A. Holte, an engineering consultant with the industrial division of Vincent Corp. Each CabinCar was to sell for $695, one-third the price of other cabin trailers on the market at that time.

Both the Canuck and the CabinCar trailer projects suffered from lack of proper market surveys and analyses. In the case of the CabinCar trailers, large commitments were made as a result of the orders placed by an American company in Texas, without sufficient investigation to establish the financial responsibility of that company. To make matters worse, the previous board had greatly increased the production plans for the Canuck aircraft without sufficient knowledge of the current market requirements. Though the Fleet workers responded with the same enthusiasm they had displayed during the war, sending some 20 trailers through the spray shop a day, the lack of buyers caused major storage problems. Two hundred CabinCars were stored under the grandstands at the Fort Erie race-track. Others were stored outside and soon began to deteriorate, as the winter weather caused joints and seams to open up. In July 1947 Tony Smith reported to the board that the plans for the CabinCar were unworkable. A total of 1,500 trailers were produced before production was stopped due to lack of buyers.

The Canuck and CabinCar failures resulted in the substantial loss of working capital. It was in this climate, in September 1947, that T.R. Harrison persuaded George C. Clarke to take over the company as president with the instructions to save the company.

George C. Clarke was the son of W. Frank Clarke C.B.E., president of Anglo-Canadian Paper Mills. Frank Clarke was a very rich man, with access to people like Bernard Baruch and Lord Beaverbrook. It was only natural that during his early career son George was involved with the pulp & paper industry, where he rose to the ranks of general sales manager for a mid-western Company in the United States. He enlisted in the RCAF and served overseas before retiring with the rank of a wing commander. Clarke was remarkably successful in his business career, being president of Reynolds Pen Canada Ltd in 1946-47, and president of Storage Wall Canada Ltd. in 1947, and president of Goldfield Uranium Mines, Structural Plastics and Duco Ltd. He was highly imaginative, charismatic and also a very persuasive salesperson.

By the time Clarke took over the company, it was $500,000 in debt, had no saleable products, no ready cash and its facilities were becoming rundown because of lack of funds for maintenance.

Clarke's job was not an easy one. He had to convince the new board of directors to give him breathing space in which to try and salvage the company, while selling off inventory to raise cash for creditors and operations. He also had to find new business to generate revenue.

Clarke reorganized the company in 1948, and its name was again changed, this time to Fleet Manufacturing Limited. During 1948 he tried to get the company work by making anything anybody wanted, including doll buggies, miniature Jeeps, and battery display racks. He even rented one of Fleet's buildings, Unit 2, to Firestone to produce much-needed money.

TWIN COACH BUSES

In 1949 Clarke was able to land a contract for assembling Twin Coach buses from parts supplied by a plant in Kent, Ohio. One of the people he recruited for this contract was Jim I. Carmicheal from Can-Car in Thunder Bay. Carmicheal came aboard in February 1948 as executive assistant to the president. He also assumed the role of plant manager. He brought with him ten-years experience in producing buses, having been with Can-Car from 1938 to 1948. He had also been chief engineer during WW II, in charge of the Curtiss Helldiver program for the United States Navy, therefore he was familiar with the aircraft business. The first coach rolled off the line in building Unit 3, in 17 working days, a considerable achievement. With a team of 98 production workers, the company was able to complete six coaches in five working days. But they soon ran into trouble getting delivery of parts such as motors and axles. To relieve this problem, they decided to produce some of the parts themselves, and they did, but not for long, as they were losing money on the project.

SHIPBOARD FURNITURE

A contract was also obtained for producing aluminum marine furniture for the Ming Sund Company in China, whose ships were being fitted out at Lauzon, Quebec. Fleet produced furniture for three complete ships from chart room to galley, as well as various pieces of furniture for eight other ships. This contract launched the company into production of other aluminum products.

FLEETLITE WINDOWS & DOORS

Fleet produced, prepackaged and assembled, 6,000 aluminum windows and 26,000 doors. The initial order was from the Canadian Mortgage & Housing Corporation, who purchased the units from Fleet and supplied them free to selected builders who were trying to meet the postwar demand for housing. This activity provided employment for returning servicemen, recent immigrants and Canadians dislocated by the shut-down of defence plants. The production rate rose to 150-200 a day. The total orders for Fleetlite windows were increased to 75,000 and a retroactive price increase was obtained to prevent the program from losing too much money, even though the design of the windows allowed it to be modified for production cost reductions.

Urban bus manufactured by Fleet for Twin Coach Corporation. – *B. MacRitchie Collection*

The postwar aluminum boat called the Car Topper manufactured by Fleet for Feather Craft.
– *B. MacRitchie Collection*

Also, the woodshop in Unit 3 began to make wooden display cabinets for Firestone. The company was soon able to take Unit 2 back from Firestone and branch into the manufacture of Bo-Peep baby cribs and Junior beds. A total of 2,500 units were made.

ASTRAL REFRIGERATORS

During 1949 Fleet was able to obtain a contract to produce small Astral refrigerators for the baby-boom market. The Company produced 30,000 in all and achieved a rate of 200 a day in 1950. The contract was completed in July 1951.

The situation at Fleet as it began its third decade is aptly summarized in a quote from a management paper prepared in August 1952 for President George D. Clarke by D.R. Cleveland, R.B. Simpson, J.O. Dibbs, W.F. Clarke and J.I. Carmichael.

"As a result of these activities (described above), at the end of 1947-48 year Fleet had lost $360,000 learning to do business, and in the year 1948-49 made a net profit of $162,000. At this stage it could be truly said that Fleet had turned the corner and the management had every reason to believe that the company would soon attain a favourable operation. The 1949-50 year saw the start of the Korean War or Conflict and the beginning of material shortages especially two key materials particularly needed by Fleet, namely steel and aluminum which began to disappear from the market. In spite of the additional capital which was raised, and offset by learning losses, during this period, the company suffered from grave shortage of working capital which precluded it from doing the required forward planning, organizing and staffing to meet the future demands of new business."

Near the end of 1947 Fleet was able to land a subcontract with de Havilland to make 120 fuselage panels and wing assemblies for the very popular de Havilland DHC-2 Beaver. The making of parts for other aircraft manufacturers would become Fleet's lifeblood in the following decades.

VI

THE THIRD DECADE 1950-59

The third decade at Fleet began as a fight for survival. Even though the company had products such as the Astral fridge in production, the outlook was not good. For example, in an effort to raise cash for a particularly difficult payday, Fleet was forced to sell residual tooling and five sets of Canuck aircraft parts for about $3,500. The following appeared in the management report mentioned in the last chapter.

"By the fall of 1950, it was apparent to Mr. Clarke that insufficient material would be available to maintain commercial lines. An executive decision was made to seek out defence business due to the climate created by the Korean Conflict. The Aircraft Production Division in Ottawa was approached and they were given a commitment in early 1951 for sub-contract work on the new AVRO Canada CF-100 jet fighter."

Fleet also tried to obtain other orders in the States. With these possibilities, it was imperative that they hold on to a nucleus of staff, so that they could obtain further defence contracts in the future. But by July 1951 the Astral contract was completed, and by August the number of employees had dropped to 125, even though in the spring of 1951 the company had been successful in obtaining a major contract worth $2.5 million to manufacture mechanical components for a large Northern Electric Company radar antenna. Subsequently, negotiations commenced with Canadian General Electric Company for similar work on one of their radar units, another $2.5 million contract. These radar units were for the Pine Tree Line which was under construction in Canada for NORAD.

By the end of May indications were very strong that Glenn L. Martin Company was serious about placing an order for wings for the Canberra bomber. However, Fleet's financial position had further deteriorated. When Fleet executives met with Defence Coordinator Mr. Crawford Gordon, they were told that the American order could not be considered and that, in view of the commitments made by the government, arrangements would need to be made to provide Fleet with financial assistance.

If the present shareholders could raise enough money to pay off Fleet's outstanding creditors, then the government would agree to provide a revolving fund of working capital assistance to the extent of $500,000. New provisions would also be made for supplying capital assistance for machine tools. This agreement required that a government representative be stationed at Fleet to countersign all cheques in order to insure that the financing provided was being used for government defence contracts.

After these arrangements were concluded Fleet received letters of intent from both Canadian General Electric for the mechanical components for the radar antennas for installation in the Pine Tree Line and with AVRO Canada, for CF-100 flaps, ailerons, wing extensions and 6,000 rocket pods for the 2.5-inch folding-fin rockets. Also, negotiations with de Havilland were successful and a contract was given for Beaver fuselage, wing panels and skis, involving additional working capital financing to the extent of $300,000, repayable towards the end of the contract. In addition a capital assistance grant of $700,000 was obtained from the government. During this period a contract was signed with Republic Aircraft to make nose-wheel undercarriage drag-links for the F-84 Thunder Jet.

With these contracts Fleet had to expand its work force very rapidly, from 125 personnel in August 1951 to over 1,100 by May 1952. This put a great deal of pressure on the administrative and supervisory staff, both to control the existing operations and to prepare for the commencement of the AVRO program. Even though this program was delayed, it would eventually require large-scale employment.

Clarke strengthened various departments and reorganized the company to accommodate this increase in personnel. He also made some public statements, perhaps exaggerated in the newspapers, about Fleet turning the corner and the company's assured future due to government guarantees. These statements were misinterpreted by Ottawa and Wood-Gordon was commissioned to do an organizational study of Fleet in August- September. The outcome of this government review was a threatened withdrawal of guarantees unless a more competent management was installed. This resulted in the placing of a management contract with Canadair and the removal of the previous management group, except for Jim Carmichael. Mr. Daniel Robertson was appointed president in 1952. The first contract of the Beaver program was completed in December. However, with the Canadair management connection, Fleet was awarded a subcontract to build F-86 Sabre wing panels, rear fuselages, and trailing edges for Canadair. A contract associated with the overhaul of Lancaster cowling, and undercarriage doors was also obtained. (These were used in the conversion of the Lancaster X bombers for air-sea rescue, anti-submarine and reconnaissance service.) Additionally Fleet built the following: fibreglass toboggans for the Canadian Army, aluminum gangplanks for Imperial Oil Co., custom windows, kitchens, bars for the commercial market, and sheet-metal jackets for furnaces.

In 1953 Mr. Herman L. Eberts was made president and the lone member of the old Fleet executive Jim Carmicheal, found it increasingly difficult to defend the past and operate under the present conditions. He resigned in March 1953. This was also the year when Fleet completed the 200th sets of fuselage and wing panels for de Havilland DHC-2 Beaver.

While under Canadair's management, Fleet bought or was given all Canadair's plastic shop and fibreglass equipment. This allowed Fleet the capability to make custom parts for F-86, T-33, C-47, D-3, North Star, and C-54 aircraft, parts such as radomes, fin and rudder tips, canopies and other similar fibreglass, phenolic and clear plastic parts.

The first autoclave for bonding plastic components was installed in 1955. It was 17 feet long, 4 feet in diameter and was capable of operating at 450° F and 75 psi. This new capability was to become one of Fleet's major strengths in future decades, when composite materials were developed for aircraft components.

Fleet remained under Canadair management from 1953 to 1959 with Eberts as president. A profit was made in 1953 and 1954 but losses were incurred in 1955, 1956 and 1957. This was due in part to lengthy waits while contracts were negotiated and awarded. One of those contracts, awarded in 1954-55, was for components for the Canadian-built CS2F-1 Tracker aircraft being built by de Havilland for the Royal Canadian Navy. Fleet made the bomb-bay doors and hatch covers.

HELIO (FLEET) H-391B COURIER

During 1954 Fleet Manufacturing Ltd. obtained the Canadian and British Commonwealth manufacturing and sales rights to the Helio H-391B Courier. Fleet was also contracted to manufacture airframe components for Helio assembly and sale in the United States and world markets.

The Courier was produced by the Helio Aircraft Company of Norwood, Massachusetts. It was developed by Dr. Otto C. Koppen of the Massachusetts Institute of Technology and Dr. Lynn Bollinger of Harvard University as a light aircraft with exceptional short takeoff and landing, with low-speed handling characteristics. The experimental prototype first flew on April 8, 1949. It was a rebuilt Piper Vagabond.

The Courier was a high-wing cantilever monoplane with Handley Page-type automatic slats on 87 percent of the leading edge and a very generous NACA type slotted all-metal flap

Earlier version of the Helio Courier in U.S. Army markings with a fabric covered rear fuselage rather than stress-skinned construction. – *B. MacRitchie Collection*

An American registered Helio Courier N242B manufactured jointly by Helio Aircraft Corporation and Fleet Manufacturing Ltd. – *B. MacRitchie Collection*

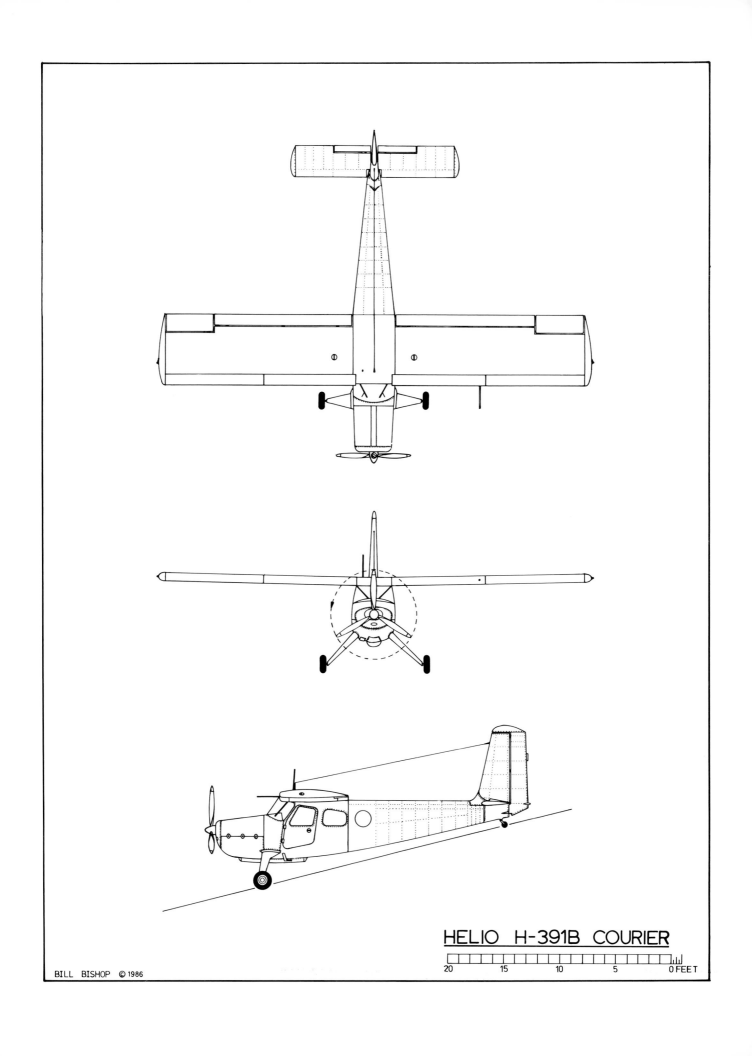

HELIO H-391B COURIER

20   15   10   5   0 FEET

on 74 percent of the trailing edge of the wing. Interceptor blades (vortex generators) were provided on the wing forward of the ailerons for good lateral control even beyond stall. An all-flying horizontal tail was fitted. These various lift improvement devices enabled the Courier to take-off and land in less than 200 feet and clear a 50-foot obstacle in less than 500 feet on take-off, and to maintain a minimum flying speed of 30 mph in powered level flight.

The fuselage was of all-metal construction. The four-place cabin section was a steel structure using the over-strength design as per Cornell University Crash and Survival Research findings, and was covered with aluminum skin. The rest of the fuselage was aluminum semi-monocoque construction, and Fleet-designed fibreglass doors, wing-tips, empennage tips and tail fairing were incorporated. Fleet had started to use the Canadair plastic shop to its advantage, creating its own design applications.

The landing gear was fixed-wheel type, with forward positioning of the main gear near the nose of the aircraft to eliminate the possibility of nose-over on rough fields, mud or snow. The Courier also had provision for floats and skis.

Fleet built airframes for three aircraft, which were shipped to Helio Aircraft for final assembly. A fourth airframe was assembled by Fleet Aircraft at Fort Erie, the Courier being registered as CF-IBF. It was test-flown by Dennis H. Byron on February 1, 1955. Extensive demonstration flying was carried out during 1955-57 for potential civil and military customers. The Courier failed to attract buyers and was finally sold to Airmart Courier & Sales Ltd. of Edmonton, Alberta, in May 1957. Courier CF-IBF was later exported to the United States. The success of the de Havilland Beaver program may have been the reason for the lack of sales.

Fleet Manufacturing was encountering continuing financial difficulties and the agreement with Helio Aircraft was cancelled. Two additional aircraft sets of parts, rather than components, were supplied to Helio for assembly, ending Fleet's entry in the executive and industrial aircraft field.

HELIO (FLEET) COURIER DATA

Engine:
    250 hp Lycoming GO-435-C2B
    six cylinder, horizontally-opposed
Dimensions:
    Wing Span – 39 ft.
    Length – 30 ft.
    Wing Area – 231 ft.

Performance
    Max. Speed – 157 mph
    Cruise Speed @ 8,500 feet – 130 mph
    Service Ceiling – 25,600 ft.
    Rate of Climb – 1,100 ft/min.
Weights:
    Gross Weight (Normal) – 2,800 lb.

DOMAN-FLEET LZ-5 HELICOPTER

Fleet's management (still under Canadair contract), recalling the days when the company manufactured and marketed a renowned line of products identified with its own name, decided that Fleet's well-being — in fact, its survival — must of necessity be based on something more substantial than a manufacturing program dependent on the nation's current defence requirements. Fleet had to have its own product. But the company's financial status precluded any possibility of being able to fund its own project. Fleet needed to associate itself with a progressive design-and-development organization in the United States, preferably one which had a promising product that required production facilities.

The end product had to be one whose market potential would be in direct ratio to Canada's expanding economy. From the many discussions concerning the choice of a suitable product, the helicopter emerged as a natural for both Fleet and Canada.

Members of the Fleet management team approached U.S. helicopter designers and manufacturers. Manufacturers realized the potential of the helicopter in Canada and were eager to participate in Fleet's plans. But Fleet had a great deal more to learn about the

Fleet Manufacturing Ltd. display at a trade show dominated by the Helio Courier tail cone and the Doman – Fleet helicopter blade and rotor hub. On display are also many of the other sub-components that Fleet was manufacturing for other aircraft companies.

– *B. MacRitchie Collection*

helicopter business. It was necessary to investigate the controversy between single rotor and other rotor configurations (tandem, intermeshing, etc.) in order to decide upon the most suitable configuration and type of helicopter for use in Canada. Fleet also had to assess how design trends might dictate the future, as well as problems with servicing and maintaining these complicated aircraft.

Fleet's president and general manager, Herman L. Eberts, accompanied by Vic Symonds and Chief Engineer Harry Louis, travelled extensively throughout Canada and the United States to conduct a comprehensive survey of such matters with many manufacturers and operators. The survey revealed that the Doman Model LZ-5, with its new and improved four-bladed, hingeless rotor system, had most of the basic features they felt would be required on a helicopter designed for Canadian and Commonwealth needs. In addition, Doman had on the drawing boards a helicopter of considerably increased capacity and improved performance, which would provide an acceptable answer to certain military requirements.

Doman Helicopters Incorporated was formed in New York City in 1945 by Gliden S. Doman, a young progressive engineer. Doman designed and developed a two-place helicopter with a hingeless, four-bladed rotor system. The new Doman rotor and control system was tested on a Sikorsky Model H-6 borrowed from the U.S. Army. Doman received considerable attention from U.S. military officials, who were impressed with the smooth operation and stability of the Doman rotor. Construction of the first all-Doman helicopter, the LZ-3, commenced in January 1949, at Danbury, Connecticut. (Doman had established his factory in Danbury in the autumn of 1947.) A market evaluation led to the development of the LZ-4, which retained many of the physical parts of the LZ-3, but featured an increase in both horsepower and rotor diameter. The LZ-4 was an experimental prototype.

Doman felt that for real success the helicopter industry required an improvement in rotor construction. He sought inherently stable flight characteristics and hoped to give these features to a rotor weighing one half that of the hinged-rotor types, upon which the industry was so dependent. Two LZ-5s were built for the U.S. Army in the Model YH-31 configuration, as "off-the-shelf" helicopters.

In 1954 Doman Helicopters Incorporated and Fleet Manufacturing signed an agreement to form a jointly owned subsidiary known as Doman-Fleet Helicopters Limited.

The Doman-Fleet organization was licensed to manufacture and market an improved version of the Model LZ-5 in Canada and the Commonwealth, and Doman-Fleet sub-licensed Fleet Manufacturing to produce the helicopter.

One LZ-5 was manufactured in 1955 at Fort Erie with major components supplied by Doman. It was the first helicopter to go into production in Canada, with its first flight June 4, 1955. Initially, the company planned to have components such as the rotor system, and main and tail blades supplied by the Doman plant, but it was envisioned that in time complete manufacture of the airframe would be undertaken at the Fleet plant.

The helicopter was capable of carrying a Volkswagen Beetle convertible athwartship in its cargo area and could accommodate six passengers plus two pilots in its commercial arrangement.

The one aircraft that was produced carried a Canadian registration CF-IBG-X and was granted a Canadian Certificate of Airworthiness on May 10, 1956. The LZ-5 was demonstrated and flown extensively in Canada during 1956-57, but the type did not attract sufficient interest to warrant production. It was returned to Doman in the United States later in 1957, and its registration was cancelled in 1959. It eventually turned up in Italy as a project with Aeronautica Sicula. Its ultimate fate is unknown.

The Doman – Fleet before covering, demonstrating a possible use for the Army with a dummy recoilless rifle. – *B. MacRitchie Collection*

The Doman – Fleet helicopter carrying a Volkswagen Beetle convertible.

– B. MacRitchie Collection

Doman – Fleet Helicopter airborne. – *B. MacRitchie Collection*

The only Canadian built Doman-Fleet LZ-5 helicopter registered as CF-IBG-X, with the staff and management in front, which gives an indication of the size of the helicopter.

– B. MacRitchie Collection

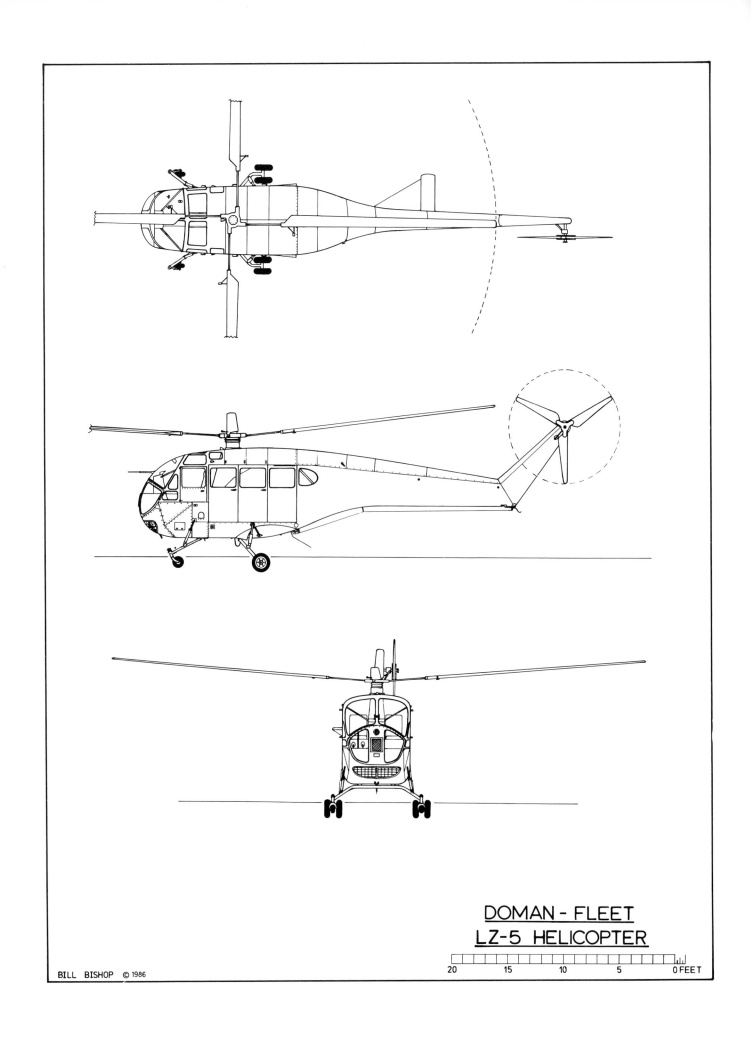

DOMAN - FLEET
LZ-5 HELICOPTER

20   15   10   5   0 FEET

DOMAN-FLEET LZ-5 DATA

Engine:
    400 hp Lycoming S.O.580-D eight-cylinder

Dimensions:
    Main Rotor Diameter – 48 ft.
    Disc Area – 1,810 sq.ft.
    Tail Rotor Diameter – 9 ft.
    Fuselage Length – 38 ft.

Performance:
    Max. Speed – 85 kts (98 mph)
    Cruise Speed – 75 kts (86 mph)
    Service Ceiling – 13,000 ft.

Hovering Ceiling
    – no ground effect – 4,000 ft.
    – in ground effect – 8,000 ft.
Range – 170 miles
Endurance – 2.4 hours

Weights:
    Empty Weight – 2,860 lb.
    Gross Weight – 5,000 lb.
    Useful Load – 2,140 lb.

In 1956 Fleet tried its hand at manufacturing aluminum car-top boats, using its expertise in handling aluminum, and though a considerable number were produced the product line was short-lived.

In 1957 Masters Smith & Company Ltd. acquired effective control of Fleet, and in December of the same year, arrangements were made to sell the bulk assets of the company to de Havilland Aircraft of Canada Ltd. for a sum of $830,000. This proposal was defeated for lack of a two-thirds majority at a special Fleet Board meeting on February 3, 1958.

The year 1958 saw Fleet still producing components for AVRO Canada's CF-100 and starting to do some significant work for the AVRO Arrow, manufacturing the instrumentation spline which ran along the back of the plane. The spline was made using honeycomb construction techniques.

Fleet's finances were improving in 1959 (having a loss of only $3,163 the previous year), when Prime Minster Diefenbaker's government announced the termination of the AVRO Arrow and Orenda Engines Iroquois programs on February 20. Fleet Aircraft suffered more of a blow from the cancellation of the AVRO Arrow than did most other subcontract companies, as Fleet was still smarting from three consecutive money losing years. In the worst year, 1957, the company lost $149,273 and its total deficit soared to more than a half million dollars. Even though its loss for 1959 was small, it caused President George Clarke (who had returned to Fleet in 1958) to look for more diverse fields, as the company was still interested in building complete aircraft. Thus on June 12, 1959, Fleet acquired the subsidiary Pine Air Ltd., Fort Erie, plans to produce a twin-engined aircraft named the Super V, but this company did not become active at that time.

Fleet Super V Beech
Bonanza N4530V
– *B. MacRitchie*
Collection

The Fleet conversion of Bay Super V Beech Bonanza. It was a conversion from single to a
twin-engine aircraft. c/n SV117-D1474 registered as N457B. – *Jack McNulty Collection*

VII

THE EPILOGUE – 1960 ONWARDS

W. (Bill) Baker appeared on the Fleet scene as general manager in 1960, becoming a vice-president in 1964. Baker had been the flight engineer on the famous Avro Aircraft Jetliner test program from 1949-51 and came to Fleet from Garrett Manufacturing. The number of employees at Fleet at that time, varied between 150 and 200, a relatively small group compared to the employee roster in the company's heyday.

Fleet acquired two product lines in 1961, the Dumont Aluminum Products and the rights to the Beechcraft Bonanza Super V program from Hammond Aircraft Company, San Francisco, California.

The Fleet arrangement to buy Dumont was complicated, convoluted, and leaves the reader wondering "Who's on First." An agreement was reached in December 1960 between Fleet Manufacturing Ltd., Isadore Hoffman and Harold Beck to purchase Dumont Aluminum Products and a number of affiliated and subsidiary concerns. Fleet agreed to pay $330,000 cash on closing, of which amount the vendors agreed to direct $180,000 to be paid to the Ava Acceptance Corporation Ltd., a concern owned by the vendors. Fleet gave the vendor the promissory note for $50,000 bearing interest at 7 percent per annum for a term of two years and also issued 500,000 shares of Fleet Manufacturing at a declared value of $200,000. These shares were to be held in escrow for five years but could be released from escrow at the rate of 2,000 shares per week, 90 days after closing. The voting rights of the escrowed shares were vested with the president of Fleet, George Clarke.

FLEET – SUPER V

Though Fleet had been shying away from complete aircraft manufacturing and had been concentrating on manufacturing aircraft components for other companies, arrangements were made in 1961 to move to Fort Erie the conversion and modification program of the Beechcraft Bonanza. The Super V, as the modified aircraft was called, was being produced primarily for the U.S. market.

The plan to convert the Bonanza from a single-engine to a light twin-engined aircraft originated from David Peterson, chief pilot for an oil company. Design and engineering work was started in 1955 by Peterson Skyline Manufacturing Company of Tulsa, Oklahoma. In 1959 rights to manufacture the Super V were obtained by Hammond Aircraft Company's subsidiary, Bay Aviation Services. In 1960 Fleet Aircraft was appointed as the Canadian and Eastern U.S. distributor for the Super V.

The actual conversion of the first Super V began and the Federal Aviation Agency (FAA) type certification was granted in 1960. The aircraft had been taken from the drawing board to final FAA certification at a cost of $1.2 million, but the project floundered after that. To help sales, Pan American World Airways pilot "Chuck" Banfe flew a Super V around the world between October 15 and 24, 1960. The basic conversion program for the Super V was moved to Fleet Aircraft at Fort Erie, where work started in January 1962. Fleet also formed the subsidiary company Fleet Aircraft Ltd. during this period to explore the feasibility of producing at low cost a light aircraft for sale in the United States.

Gordon Schwartz was appointed head of Fleet's Super V program and Randy Lans, who worked on the original prototype in California, was brought in as project engineer. Although the twin-engined aircraft was created from the airframe and wing sections of the Bonanza, the modifications were extensive enough to require recertification as a new aircraft. The wings and fuselage were greatly strengthened; engine mountings had to be designed for the wing, a fibreglass fairing covered the nose; the additional space was used for baggage; and the leading edge of each wing was sealed to provide integral tanks for an additional 30 gallons of fuel.

Fleet spent over 2,000 hours revamping the original demonstrator. Modifications included new streamlined engine cowlings for the Lycoming O-360-A1D engines (which had replaced the Lycoming A1B fuel-injection engines), a nose-cone for a landing light, better soundproofing, an improved entry door, and a revised instrument panel. Canadian certification was also obtained for the aircraft. As this was considered a new aircraft, not a converted twin Bonanza, and as the company was not in the conversion business, Schwartz stated clearly, "If you have a single Bonanza and want a twin, we will sell you a Super V and take the Bonanza as a trade-in, just as we would any other plane."

Marketing plans for the Fleet Super V were put in place and sales demonstration tours were conducted. Fleet negotiated with distributors in the United States and picked the Buffalo Aeronautical Corporation, Buffalo, New York, as their first distributor. However, only five new Super Vs were built by Fleet in Canada, though they rebuilt the original "Around the World" Super V. Two Super Vs were sold to private owners in the United States through the company's wholly owned United States sales outlet, Fleet Aircraft Inc. Lack of additional sales, due to intense competition at the end of 1963, forced Fleet to sell the Super V program and inventory, including three complete Super V aircraft, to Mitchell Trimotor Aircraft Corporation of Savannah, Georgia. A total of 14 Super Vs were built in Canada and the United States, including two which were rebuilt. Thus ended the last of Fleet's complete aircraft ventures for many decades.

FLEET – SUPER V DATA

Engine:
   Two 180 hp Lycoming O-360-A1D
   4-cylinder horizontally opposed piston engines.
Dimensions:
   Wing Span – 32 feet, 10 in.
   Length – 25 feet, 1 in.
   Wing Area – 181 sq. ft.

Performance:
   Max. Speed – 210 mph
   Cruise Speed – 190 mph
   Service Ceiling – 20,000 feet
   Rate of Climb – 1,550 ft./min.
Weights:
   Gross Weight – 3,400 lb.
   Empty Weight – 2,200 lb.

In an effort to ensure its survival, Fleet expanded into varied and diversified projects in the 1960s. The following is a brief review of that period with highlights of some of the major company events during that decade.

On June 20, 1961, Fleet changed the name Doman-Fleet to Dumont Aluminum Limited, Hamilton, Ontario. by supplementary letters patent. This company made storm windows, awnings and siding, mainly for the booming housing market.

Orders were obtained from General Electric of Syracuse, New York, for heat-exchanger cabinets to house transducer modules for sonar systems and staves as supports for ships' hull mounted sonar domes. In 1962 the company acquired the fixed assets of Richardson Boat Company, which proved to an unsuccessful venture. This was the same company that Avro had tried to diversify into after the Arrow cancellation. Later in the year, Fleet acquired assets of a foundry at Haley, Ontario, which produced special alloys. This foundry was previously owned by the Crown and operated by Light Alloys Company Ltd., was a subsidiary of Dominion Magnesium Limited., Toronto. Fleet renamed the company Haley Industries Limited. In January 1963 Fleet Manufacturing Limited purchased all of the outstanding shares of W.H.G. Estates Ltd., Hamilton. With its name changed to Ronark Development Ltd., it became a holding company for the following subsidiaries: Ronark Development

Eastern Ltd., operating as a builder in Hamilton; A.B. Taylor Construction Ltd. in Ottawa, a building constructor; W.H.Grisenthwaite Developments Ltd. of Hamilton, a real estate holding and development concern; and Craftex Homes, (Western) Ltd., also of Hamilton, a speculative builder.

During September Fleet sold the assets of Dumont Aluminum Products to Shully's Industries Ltd. for $850,000 in cash, for once making a profit.

Fleet Manufacturing received orders from de Havilland Aircraft of Canada to produce ailerons for the Douglas DC-9 airliner during 1964. De Havillands at that time was operating the old Avro plant at Malton, producing complete wing assemblies for the Douglas Aircraft Company in the States.

In 1965 Bill Baker left Fleet to become president of McDonnell Douglas Canada in Ottawa.

As a result of the installation in 1965 of the large (26 feet long, 8 feet diameter) Devine autoclave in Unit 4, more subcontract work came Fleet's way in September 1966. Grumman Aircraft Engineering Corporation awarded Fleet the contract for work on the honeycomb and metal-bonded components for the A-6A Intruder U.S. Navy medium-range naval bomber. Canadian Westinghouse Company entered a $600,000 contract with Fleet to produce the handling gear for launch, tow and recovery of a variable-depth sonar system which was to be installed on the HMCS Bras D'Or, the Canadian Navy's experimental hydrofoil ship.

During 1967 orders were received from Douglas Aircraft for 100 sets of flaps and 70 sets of ailerons for DC-9 production. This order was worth $1,654,000. It was during 1967 that Fleet delivered the 200th DC-9 aileron set, from a contract started in 1964. Other contracts came in for components for the de Havilland Canada DHC-5 Buffalo aircraft. This was a tactical transport being produced by DHC for the Brazilian Air Force and the Canadian military. The first issue of the company's new in-house newsletter, *Fleet Forum,* was issued this year, replacing the defunct newsletter *Plane Talk*, first issued in 1942.

Subcontract work with Grumman Aircraft Corporation continued with the awarding of a contract worth $528,000. This contract was for more bonded components, 78 sets of nine metal-bonded parts consisting of three deck covers and six fin-panel assemblies. Fleet was now making 25 parts for the A-6A Intruder aircraft for the U.S. Navy. At this time Fleet Manufacturing started production of 2900 series floats for Cessna 180 aircraft. These unique floats were produced from urethane foam and had a fibreglass skin.

During 1968 Fleet received additional orders from Grumman for flap trailing edges for the A-6A Intruder Bomber thus bringing the number of parts that it was making for this aircraft to 32. Additional orders were also received from General Electric for more heat-exchanger cabinets and staves. An order for 26 sets of APD-7 Side Looking Radar was placed by Westinghouse's Defence and Space Centre, Baltimore, Maryland. The new radar was installed in the RA-5C Vigilante aircraft. Fleet anticipated future orders for the more advanced APD-8 radar for the Grumman F-111D fighter/bomber series of aircraft.

In 1969 Fleet received a contract from Hughes Aircraft for floats for the Hughes 500 helicopter. The floats were made of thermoplastic, each weighing 50 pounds, as compared to the traditional air-bag-type floats which weighed over 120 pounds each.

Lockheed Aircraft placed an order with Fleet Manufacturing for producing the No. 2 engine nacelle, aft dorsal structure and main landing gear doors for the new wide-body Lockheed Tri-Star L-1011 Airbus passenger aircraft. To accommodate these large orders, a major expansion took place between Units 2 & 3, resulting in a floor space increase of 21,000 square feet. This expansion was to accommodate numerically-controlled machine tools such as the Kearney Milwaukee-Matic and Sunderstrand Omnimill. The Research & Development department organized a program to investigate and develop composite-material bonding and honeycomb structures in conjunction with the government's Defence Research Board and the research facilities of the Institute of Aerospace Studies at the University of Toronto.

This work made Fleet a leader in honeycomb construction and the production of composite-material components for many North American aircraft manufacturers. The honeycomb work led to the construction of a special facility dedicated to the production of satellite bodies for the Hughes Aircraft Company. Some of these satellites were launched from the NASA shuttle. Fleet had come from biplanes to the space age in 60 years.

Today, Fleet is known as Fleet Industries, a division of Fleet Aerospace Corporation, and the company continues its successful, high quality subcontract work, making large and small components for many aircraft manufacturing customers and defence contractors.

Though the recent decades of Fleet's history and it's accomplishments, have been treated rather lightly, the intent of this book was to really record the flying years of Fleet.

Fleet then and now. A restored Fleet 7 under the tail of a Air Canada Boeing 747.

– *B. MacRitchie Collection*

APPENDIX I

SUMMARY OF FLEET BUILT AIRCRAFT

MODEL	NAME	NO. BUILT
2/7	FLEET 2	7
7	FAWNS I & II	71
10	FLEET 10	122
16	FINCH I & II	427
21	MODEL 21	11
50	FREIGHTER	5
60	FORT I & II	101
PT-26/PT-23	CORNELL II	1902
80	CANUCK	225
H-391B	HELIO COURIER	1
LZ-5	DOMAN-FLEET HELICOPTER	1
	FLEET SUPER V	5
	TOTAL	2877

APPENDIX II

PRODUCTS MANUFACTURED BY FLEET

Product Description	No. of Units
Fleet CabinCar Trailers	1,500
Assembly of Twin Coach City Transit Buses	?
Aluminum Marine Furniture	11 shipsets
Hotel Bureau Desks	1,500
Fleetlite Aluminum Windows	75,000
Fleetwood Windows	6,000
Fleet Dor-paks	26,000
Asssorted Wooden Nursery Furniture	2,500
Astral Refrigerators	30,000
Metal Transfer Cases	4,000
Display Cases	?
Fibreglass Toboggans for Canadian Army	?
Aluminum Gangways for Imperial Oil Co. Canada	?
Fibreglass Boats	?
Aluminum Car-Top Boats	?
Metal Custom Kitchen and Bars (commercial)	?
Sheet Metal Jackets for Furnaces	?
Office Partitions	?
Radar Antennas & Tower Components for Canadian General Electric Co., Toronto	?
Radar & Microwave Antennas for Northern Electric Co., Belleville	?
Radar Antennas and Towers for General Electric, Syracuse	?
Nose-wheel Drag Link for F-84 Aircraft	?
Wings & Fuselage Panels for DHC-2 & L-20	200
Avro Lancaster X Outer Wings	299
Trailing Edges	349
Elevators	292
Cowlings & Doors for Avro Lancaster	?
Tooling for Ford, Orenda & Thor	?
Canadair F-86 Sabre Centre Wing Box,	?
Wing Panels, Leading & Trailing Edges, & Rear Fuselage Components	?
Avro CF-100 Wing Extensions, Flaps, Ailerons, Dive Brakes	?
CF-100 Rocket Pods	6,000
DHC-4 Caribou Honeycomb Components for Doors, Walkways	340
Sonar System Staves And Heat Exchangers for General Electric, Syracuse	?

APPENDIX III

THE HISTORY OF
THE FLEET COMPANY NAME & PRESIDENTS

1923 May 29   CONSOLIDATED AIRCRAFT CORPORATION –
                        President Major R.H. Fleet

1929 February   FLEET AIRCRAFT INCORPORATED
                        President Major R.H. Fleet

1929 July   CONSOLIDATED AIRCRAFT CORPORATION – FLEET
                        President Major R.H. Fleet

1930 March 25   FLEET AIRCRAFT of CANADA LIMITED
                        President Captain Jack Sanderson - 1930 - 1942

1936 November 17   FLEET AIRCRAFT LIMITED
                        (wholly owned Canadian subsidiary)
1942   President E.G. McMillan
1943   President E.G. Smith

1946 July   FLEET MANUFACTURING AND AIRCRAFT LIMITED
                        President Norman Vincent
1947   President George D. Clarke

1948 August   FLEET MANUFACTURING LIMITED

1952   President Daniel Robertson
1953   President Hermann L. Eberts
1957   President Daniel Robertson
1958   President George D. Clarke
1965   President Ronald K. Fraser

1973 February 1   FLEET INDUSTRIES
                        (A Division of Ronyx Corporation)
                        President Ronald K. Fraser

1983   President A. George Dragone of
                        FLEET AEROSPACE CORPORATION

1984 March   FLEET INDUSTRIES
1990   (A Division of Fleet Aerospace Corporation)

BIBLIOGRAPHY

Andre, John M., *"U.S. Military Aircraft Designations and Serials Since 1909"*, Leicester, United Kingdom, 1979.

Bettinger, Fred, J., letter "Convair History," August 1973, unpublished.

Cumming, Bill, "Fleet Model 50 Freighter", *Wingspan*, Jan/Feb. 1989.

Cumming, Bill, "Fleet 80 Canuck", *Canadian General Aviation News*, Dec. 1986.

Cumming, Bill, "Fleet Fort", *Air Progress Warbirds International*, Summer, 1987.

Durosko, Ted, "The Fleet Super V," unknown source.

"Fleet Forum", Fleet Industries Newsletter, Fort Erie, Ontario, 1967-87.

Fleet Aircraft, Manufacturing, Industries, Annual Reports, 1935-1987.

Fort Erie Times Review, Fort Erie, Ontario, 1929-42.

Gordon, David, *"Of Men and Planes"*, VOL. III, Ottawa, 1968.

Godfrey, David, "Score Sheet on the Half-Century," *Canadian Aviation*, Toronto, Ontario, 1978.

Martland, Barrie, "Fleet Shows Fighting Form," *Canadian Aviation*, Toronto, Ontario, December 1962.

McIntyre, M.L., "The Fleet 50 Freighter," *Canadian Aviation Historical Society Journal"*, Toronto, Ontario, Spring 1969.

Milberry, L., *"Aviation in Canada"*, McGraw-Hill Ryerson Ltd., Toronto, Ontario, 1979.

Molson, K.M., & Taylor, H.A., *"Canadian Aircraft since 1909"*, Canada's Wings, Sittsville, Ontario, 1982.

Page, R.D. et al (ARROWHEADS), *"Avro Arrow CF 105"*, The Boston Mills Press, Erin, Ontario, 1980.

Page, R.D., *"Avro Canuck CF 100 All Weather Fighter"*, The Boston Mills Press, Erin, Ontario, 1981. 2nd Edition, 1990.

Page, R.D., *"Canada's Flying Museum, Canadian Warplane Heritage Museum"*, 2nd Edition, The Boston Mills Press, Erin, Ontario, 1987.

Page, Bette, *"Mynarski's Lanc, The Story of Two Famous Lancaster Bombers KB726 & FM213"*, The Boston Mills Press, Erin, Ontario, 1989.

"PLANE TALK," *"Fleet Company Newsletter"*, 1942.

Shortt, A.J., *"Fleet Model 21"*, National Aviation Museum, Ottawa, Ont. 1977.

Shortt, A.J., *"Doman-Fleet LZ-5"*, National Aviation Museum, Ottawa, Ont. 1978.

Shortt, A.J., *"Helio H-391B Courier"*, National Aviation Museum, Ottawa, Ontario, 1978.

Shortt, A.J., *"Fleet Canuck"*, National Aviation Museum, Ottawa, Ontario, 1981.

Shortt, A.J., *"Fleet Freighter"*, National Aviation Museum, Ottawa, Ont. 1981.

Shortt, A.J., *"Fleet Model 60K Fort"*, National Aviation Museum, Ottawa, Ont. 1981.

Shortt, A.J., *"Fleet Trainers"*, National Aviation Museum, Ottawa, Ontario, 1983.

Shortt, A.J., *"Those FLEET TRAINERS Models 2,7,10 & 16"*, CAHS Journal, Vol. 27, No. 4, Winter '89.

Stead, Jack L., letter, Super V Specifications, unpublished.

Vincent, C., and Fletcher, D., "The Fawn in the RCAF," *Random Thoughts*, Vol. 10, No. 10/11, IPMS Canada.

Vincent, C., and Fletcher, D., "Fleet Finch," *Random Thoughts,* Vol. 10, No. 12, IPMS Canada.

Vincent, C. "Fleet's Indefensible Fort," *High Flight*, Vol. 4 No. 2, Canada's Wings.

Weissman, Tom, "Canada's Fleet Canuck," *Private Pilot*, date unknown.

Wherry, Joseph, "The Fleet Canuck," *Air Trails Pictorial*, date unknown.

Williams, T., "My Love Affair with the Fleet 21M," *Canadian Flight Magazine*, Jan/Feb. 1979.

Unknown author, "Fleet Rotary", *Canadian Aviation Magazine,* May, 1954.

Unknown author, "Canadian Personnel for Canadian Fleets," *Canadian Aviation Magazine,* May 1931.

Unknown author G.M.R., "Fleet Progress," *Canadian Aviation Magazine*, January 1937.

The nearly completed Fleet Fort restored to flying condition by the Spirit of Fleet III team led by Bruce MacRitchie, 1988. *– B. MacRitchie Collection*